# ROLE PLAYS FOR TODAY

## Photocopiable activities to get students speaking

Jason Anderson

# Contents



## 1 Services Practical, leisure and travel

| Role Play and description | Levels | | | | | Grammar | Functions | Vocabulary |
|---|---|---|---|---|---|---|---|---|
| | Elementary | Pre-int | Intermediate | Upper int | Advanced | | | |
| **1k Complaining in a hotel**<br>Guest and hotel receptionist<br>***page 19*** | | ● | ● | ● | ● | *Will* for spontaneous decisions<br>*There is / are...* for describing rooms | Complaining<br>Providing excuses<br>Apologising | Hotels: *wake-up call, guest, reduction* |
| **1l Travel Agent**<br>Customer and travel agent<br>***page 20*** | | ● | ● | ● | | Question forms | Making enquiries<br>Clarifying details | Travel / holidays: *excursion, flight*<br>Purchasing: *per person, hire* |

# 2 **Shopping** Supermarkets, clothes and restaurants

| Role Play and description | Elementary | Pre-int | Intermediate | Upper int | Advanced | Grammar | Functions | Vocabulary |
|---|---|---|---|---|---|---|---|---|
| **2a Supermarket shopping**<br>Customer and store assistant<br>***page 22*** | ● | ● | ● | | | Countable and uncountable nouns | Enquiring about products | Food: *fresh fish, bananas, eggs*<br>Shopping: *checkout, receipt* |
| **2b Clothes shop**<br>Customer and clothes shop assistant<br>***page 24*** | ● | ● | ● | | | Demonstratives (*those, these, that, this*) | Expressing personal preferences<br>Paying compliments | Clothes: *jeans, top, shirt*<br>Shopping: *buying clothes* |
| **2c DIY shop**<br>Customer and DIY shop assistant<br>***page 26*** | | ● | ● | ● | | Preposition + gerund<br>Verb patterns | Describing an object without its name (paraphrasing)<br>Negotiating | Shapes and materials: *round, plastic*<br>DIY: *pliers* |
| **2d Shoe shop**<br>Customer and shoe shop assistant<br>***page 30*** | ● | ● | ● | | | *Too* and *enough* | Expressing personal preferences | Clothes: *suit, try on*<br>Shoes: *sandals, high heels* |
| **2e Traditional restaurant**<br>Customers and waiter<br>***page 31*** | | ● | ● | ● | | *Will* for placing orders<br>Indirect and direct question forms | Enquiring about dishes<br>Complimenting food<br>Complaining | Food: *peppers, stewed, pudding* |
| **2f Fast Food restaurant**<br>Customer and assistant<br>***page 34*** | ● | ● | | | | Contracted question forms | Placing an order<br>Complaining | Food: *fast food* |
| **2g Out of stock**<br>Customer and electronics store assistant<br>***page 36*** | | | | ● | ● | Demonstratives vs. pronouns | Reasoning with someone<br>Making suggestions<br>Apologising | Purchasing products: *model, refund*<br>Emotion adjectives: *calm, annoyed* |

| Role Play and description | Levels | | | | | Grammar | Functions | Vocabulary |
|---|---|---|---|---|---|---|---|---|
| | Elementary | Pre-int | Intermediate | Upper int | Advanced | | | |

# 3 **Social life** Going out, friends and relationships

| Role Play and description | Elementary | Pre-int | Intermediate | Upper int | Advanced | Grammar | Functions | Vocabulary |
|---|---|---|---|---|---|---|---|---|
| **3a A day out in London**<br>Groups of students decide how to spend the day<br>***page 38*** | ● | ● | ● | | | Structures for suggestions<br>Present continuous and *going to* for future intentions | Making, accepting and refusing suggestions | Free time: *going out, live performance, exhibition* |
| **3b Party strangers**<br>Two strangers introduce themselves<br>***page 40*** | | ● | ● | ● | | Various | Using formal / informal registers<br>Introducing yourself<br>Showing interest | Personal details<br>Free time: *interests*<br>Informal English: *naff, ...and stuff* |
| **3c Argument between friends**<br>Two friends argue outside a cinema<br>***page 42*** | | | ● | ● | ● | Question tags<br>Imperatives | Making and refuting accusations<br>Making up after an argument | Free time: *go out, nightclub, cinema* |
| **3d Telephone phone-around**<br>Groups of students make plans for an evening out<br>***page 44*** | | ● | ● | ● | | Present continuous and *going to* for future arrangements and intentions; *will* for new decisions | Making and declining suggestions | Social events: *go out, pub, restaurant, go clubbing* |
| **3e Flatmates**<br>Flatmates decide how to share the housework<br>***page 46*** | | ● | ● | ● | | Verb patterns (verb + gerund; verb + infinitive; preposition + gerund) | Making suggestions<br>Agreeing and disagreeing | Housework and chores: *vacuum the flat, do the washing up* |
| **3f Breaking bad news**<br>Mark phones his friend Nicky<br>***page 48*** | | ● | ● | ● | | Past simple | Breaking bad news<br>Sympathising | Pets: *feed, cage, rabbit* |
| **3g Meeting old friends**<br>Class meet up again 10 years into the future<br>***page 50*** | | ● | ● | ● | ● | Present perfect simple and continuous to describe changes | Expressing surprise<br>Paying compliments<br>Making observations | Various, including appearance, lifestyle, work, family |

# 4 **Lifestyle** Work, accommodation and education

| Role Play and description | Elementary | Pre-int | Intermediate | Upper int | Advanced | Grammar | Functions | Vocabulary |
|---|---|---|---|---|---|---|---|---|
| **4a Phoning for a job interview**<br>Job applicant and human resources manager<br>***page 52*** | | ● | ● | ● | | Question forms, both direct and indirect | Making polite enquiries<br>Describing personality | Work: *salary, position*<br>Personality adjectives: *patient, polite* |
| **4b Job interview 1**<br>Applicant and interviewer (for lower levels)<br>***page 54*** | ● | ● | | | | *Can* for ability<br>Question forms | Giving personal information | Work: *salary, CV, unemployed* |
| **4c Job interview 2**<br>Applicant and interviewer (for higher levels)<br>***page 56*** | | | ● | ● | ● | *Can* for ability<br>Present perfect for life experience<br>Question forms | Giving personal information<br>Describing personality | Work: *part-time, wages*<br>Personality adjectives: *reliable, friendly* |

# 5 Creative role plays

# Introduction

Role play activities have been a part of language teaching for many years. They are popular with teachers and students alike for several important reasons:

- They provide the spoken language practice that is vital for all language learning
- They provide us with the opportunity to take our students out of the classroom for a 'test run' of real world language use
- They allow students to become someone else for part of the lesson, and thereby to leave behind their inhibitions and worries
- They involve an element of play that provides an enjoyable contrast to the coursebook exercises and helps to develop rapport between students

*Role Plays for Today* includes both role play activities (in which the students pretend to be somebody else) and simulation activities (in which the students are themselves, but in an imaginary situation).

### Organisation of the book

The 39 units of the book are divided into five categories:

**1)** Services; Practical, leisure and travel

**2)** Shopping; Supermarkets, clothes and restaurants

**3)** Social life; Going out, friends and relationships

**4)** Lifestyle; Work, accommodation and education

**5)** Creative role plays

These categories have been chosen to enable teachers to browse for role plays that may be suitable for their classes as well as to allow fast access for teachers who know which role play they are looking for. The Contents also include an indication of what grammar, functional language and vocabulary is likely to be activated by the students in each role play. There is also an index of grammar, vocabulary and functions at the back of the book.

### Levels

Both in the Teacher's Notes and in the Contents I have indicated the range of levels at which each role play could be used. As role play activities involve the students choosing their own language and interacting with other members of the class, they are more flexible than other activities in the range of levels each one can cover. Most of the role plays are suitable for three or more levels, and nearly all are suitable for intermediate level students. However, always check the *Target language* and the complexity of a role play before taking it into class. Labels such as 'elementary', 'intermediate' and 'advanced' mean different things in different language schools around the world.

### Selecting the right role play

Remember that classes of students vary, and it's a good idea to think carefully about several factors before choosing a role play for your students:

- Will my students enjoy this role play?
- Is it at the right stage in their syllabus?
- Will they find the language practice useful?
- Is it culturally suitable?
- Will they be familiar with the situation?
- Is the rapport between the students good enough for this role play to work?

The Teacher's Notes have been kept brief to make them clear, but depending on your answers to the above questions, you may want to adapt the activity, choose a different 'lead-in' or spend time familiarising the students with an aspect of UK culture before doing the role play. If you do this, make sure you allow for more time.

## Making role plays work

When discussing the degree of success of an activity such as a role play, teachers often talk about whether the students 'got into it' or not. Most teachers have, at some time in their career, had one of those classes that seem to 'get into everything' and one of those classes that don't seem able to 'get into anything'. It does partly depend on the students, so select your role plays carefully. Nonetheless, a significant part of the responsibility for whether a role play works in class lies with the teacher. Here are a few basic tips that will improve the degree of success that any role play has.

### The lead-in

When you're leading into a role play, notice how the students are responding to the discussion questions, or the task. If they seem familiar with the context and interested in it, you can go straight into the role play. If not, take more time to get clear feedback, check vocabulary and do a demonstration before you start the role play.

### Demonstration

Demonstration is extremely useful, especially with classes that lack confidence or are at the lowest level recommended for a role play. As well as being the clearest way to instruct the activity, demonstration also provides them with a useful 'live listening' task, a model for the conversation they are going to have, and shows how the *Target language* could be used. You could get two strong students to perform the demonstration in front of the rest of the class, or, do it yourself with a student. This will enable you to show them how to mime, act and use intonation appropriately (see below). Make sure the other students are paying attention during the demonstration – you could set them a listening (or watching) task, just as you might do for a standard coursebook listening.

## Classroom dynamics

As a basic rule of thumb, ask the students to stand up if a similar conversation in 'the real world' would take place standing up (e.g. ordering at the counter of a fast food restaurant) and sit down if a similar conversation would take place seated (e.g. ordering in a traditional restaurant). If you can move the desks and the chairs, transform the central space of the classroom to simulate the 'real world' environment (e.g. two chairs facing each other across a desk for a job interview role play). If you can't move the desks or chairs, make sure the students are facing each other and interacting as naturally as possible.

## Starting the role play

If the start of the role play involves a 'first meeting' or an 'entrance', why not use the classroom door as a prop? You can send half the students out of the room to re-enter 'in role'. If the role play involves a telephone conversation, get the students to mime a 'ring-ring' to start the phone call. Get them to form a queue if they are in a post office or at immigration in an airport. If a handshake is natural in the role play context, encourage them to do this as well. These prompts often provide the necessary cue for students to get into role.

## Props and mime

A few small props can make a surprisingly big difference. Laminated menus (*Traditional restaurant*), a cardboard microphone (*TV chat show*) or business cards made by the students (*International business etiquette*) will often encourage students to involve far more body language than they otherwise would, which often improves their acting. If it would take too long to create the necessary props (e.g. *Shoe shop*), make sure that you do a demonstration that involves plenty of mime (unpacking and fitting the shoe, wafting the air to indicate smelly feet, etc.). Background music can also be a very effective prop for parties, restaurants, etc.

## Acting

Bearing in mind that, during a role play, some students will be finding it difficult enough just producing the sentences, never expect too much acting from low level classes. Conversely, if you think they will find the role play fairly easy (often at higher levels), encourage them to act it as realistically as possible. As mentioned above, a good demonstration with plenty of emotion, facial expression and body language will give the students plenty of ideas. Always remember to give students time to practise if you want them to act out their role play in front of the class.

## Intonation

Role play provides a good opportunity for students to practise using intonation effectively in context. As mentioned above, a good demonstration can bring their attention to this. In addition, focus on the *Target language* before the role play and elicit possible intonation patterns for each sentence or expression from the students. If necessary, provide and drill a model, encouraging the students to copy you as closely as possible.

## Rapport and trust in the class

Some of the role plays in the book will work much better when the class know each other well and should not be attempted in the first lesson (*Argument between friends*, for example!). Where students are being themselves (i.e. in simulation activities), they may be more reluctant to give personal information than in true role plays. So, if in doubt, give them the opportunity to be someone else. Most importantly, remember that role play is undoubtedly one of the best ways to improve rapport and trust between the students in your class.

Many thanks to all the teachers at Oxford House College and Rose of York Language School (London), The English Centre (Sassari, Italy) and numerous others who trialled material for me. I hope you have as much fun using *Role Plays for Today* as my colleagues, I myself, and our students have had during the development of the book!

# 1 Services
## Practical, leisure and travel

## 1a Tourist information office – Teacher's notes

### Time / Level

30–50 minutes / Elementary to Intermediate

### Target language

**Grammar**

Imperatives (*Take the second right.*)
*Will* for general future predictions (*You'll see it on your left.*)

**Functions**

Giving directions (*Take the third right into Park Road.*)
Making recommendations (*You could visit the castle.*)

**Vocabulary**

Tourist attractions (*castle, cathedral, funfair*)
Verbs of motion (*go straight on, turn left*)

### Preparation

Copy the directions below and the two role play cards (one of each per pair). Cut up as indicated.

### Lead-in suggestion

Put these questions on the board for discussion in pairs followed by feedback:

*In your town...*
*1) What are the most popular tourist attractions?*
*2) Where is a good place to have lunch?*
*3) Could you recommend a good hotel?*

Elicit from the students who answers these kind of questions for a job (*tourist information officer*).

### Role Play instructions

Introduce the role play, and hand out a copy of the directions below, and the Assistant's role play card with the map of Benton. Using the map, they should correct the factual mistakes (no grammar or spelling mistakes) in the text. The first has been done. Do another example if necessary. Check the answers afterwards.

**Answers**
(*in order*) ~~left~~ → right; ~~second~~ → first; ~~Street~~ → Road; ~~park~~ → beach; ~~3000~~ → 300; ~~opposite~~ → next to; ~~miles~~ → metres; ~~beach~~ → Town Square; ~~before~~ → after; ~~left~~ → right.

Hand out the role play cards to the students in pairs. If there is an odd number of students, create one group of three with two friends visiting Benton together. Give them 2–3 minutes to read through, and then point out the *Target language*. Tell the Assistants that they should invent any details that aren't on the role play card (e.g. hotel prices) and that they can show the map when giving directions. When they are ready they can begin. If any pairs finish early, the Tourist can dictate the directions back to the Assistant to check that they got them right. When they finish, they should swap cards and do Situation 2.

### Follow-up suggestion

If there is time, the students will enjoy writing and following directions for each other. Give each pair a slip of paper on which they should write directions to a place within the school / college (e.g. café, library, reception):

*Go out of the classroom and turn right...*

Monitor and correct if necessary. When they've finished they can give their written directions to another pair who can follow them, then come back and say where they got to. Find out if this was the intended place!

---

## Tourist information office

Role Plays for Today

**Look at the map of Benton, and correct the 10 mistakes in these directions:**

### How to get to Dazzle Nightclub

Go out of the office and turn ~~left~~ *right*. Go along the High Street and take the second right into Oxford Street. Go straight on until you come to The Promenade. You'll see the park in front of you. Turn left and go straight on for about 3000 metres. You'll see it on your left, opposite the Grand Hotel.

### How to get to the Car Park

Go out of the office and turn right. Go straight on, along the High Street for about 500 miles, until you come to the beach. Take the first left before the square, and it will be on your left, opposite Benton Gardens.

 

# Tourist information office



## Student A – Assistant

**You work in the Benton tourist information office. Help the tourists who come in by answering their questions, giving directions and any other information they need.**

| Tourist Attractions | Opening Times | Cost |
|---|---|---|
| Benton Cathedral | 10am – 4.30pm | Free |
| Benton Castle | 9am – 5pm | £4.20 |
| Benton Museum / Gallery | 11am – 7pm | £2.80 |
| Benton Funfair | 2pm – 10pm | £12.00 |
| Benton Gardens | 10am – 3.30pm | Free |
| The beach | All day! | Free! |

### Target language

**Giving directions**

*Go out of the office and turn right.*
*Take the first left into Oxford Road.*
*Go straight on past the hospital…*
*…until you come to the Town Square.*
*It's next to / opposite the Regent Hotel.*

**Making recommendations**

*You could visit the castle.*
*Why don't you try the Regent Hotel?*

**Other language**

*It's open from… to… It costs… (£)*

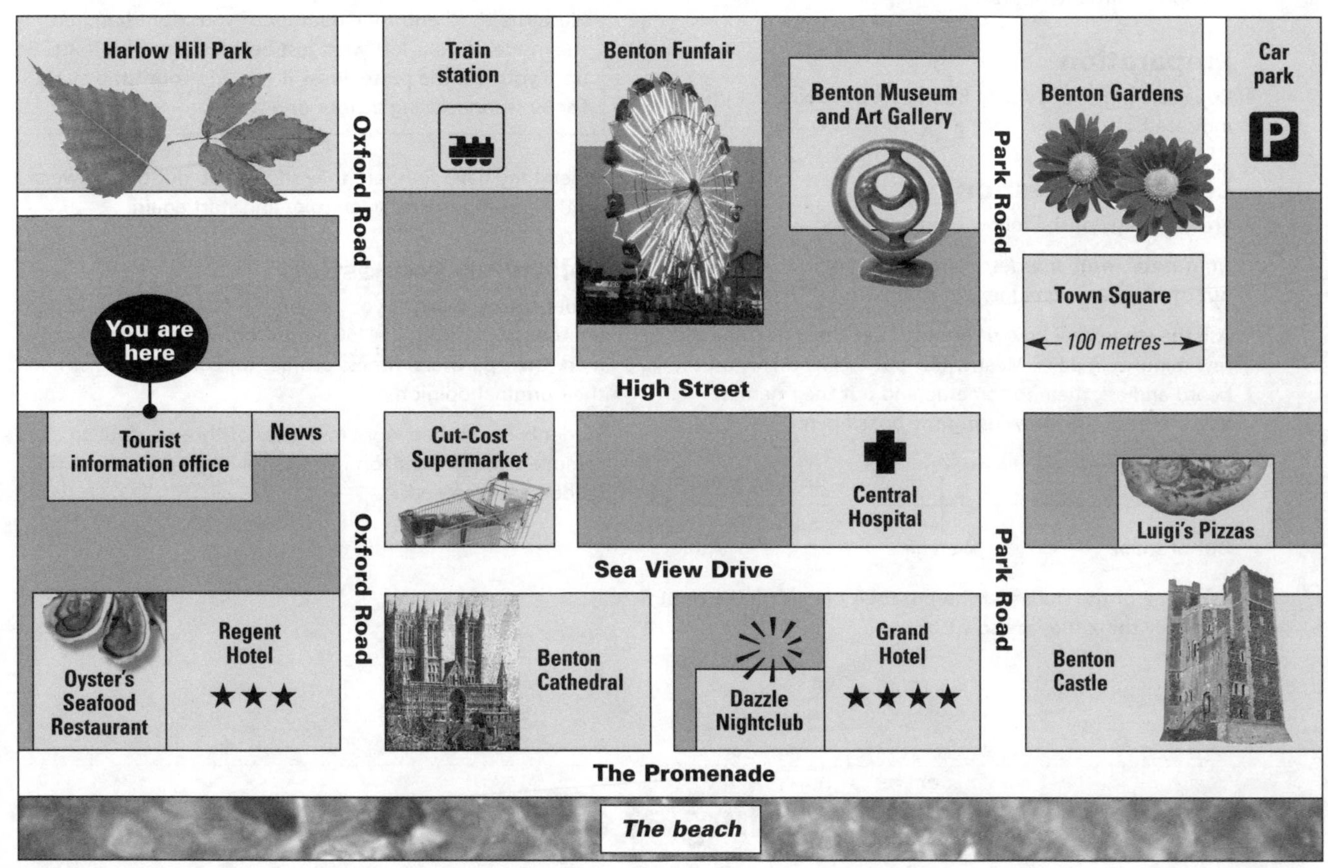


# Tourist information office

Role Plays for Today

## Student B – Tourist

**Situation 1**

You are a tourist. You are visiting Benton for a weekend. It is summer and the weather's fine. Go into the tourist information office and find out about the local tourist attractions, the best restaurants and a hotel for tonight. Don't forget to get directions, check prices and opening times for the tourist attractions! Write down the important information.

*Now swap roles.*

**Situation 2**

You are a businesswoman / businessman. You are visiting Benton for one day and one night only. You have a meeting this morning. After that, you are free. Don't forget to find a good hotel for tonight, a good restaurant for dinner, and something to do this afternoon. Money is no problem – your company is paying! Make a note of the important information.

### Target language

*I'm here for the weekend.*
*I need some information about...*
*Could you tell me…?*
*Do you have…?*
*How do I get there?*
*How far is it?*
*How much does it cost?*
*What are the opening times?*
*Could you write that down?*
*Sorry. Could you repeat that, please?*

 

# 1b Enrolling at a gym – Teacher's notes

## Time / Level

40–60 minutes / Pre-intermediate to Advanced

## Target language

**Grammar**

Adverbs and questions of frequency (*How much / many / often? Twice a week.*)

Imperatives (*Stand up, please.*)

**Functions**

Giving polite commands (*Could you measure your pulse, please?*)

Giving advice (*You should start with a little exercise and build up.*)

**Vocabulary**

Fitness / Health (*muscles, pulse, exercise*)

Sports (*athlete, sporty*)

## Preparation

Copy role play cards A and B (one set per pair). Cut up as indicated.

## Lead-in suggestion

Pre-teach any of the following if necessary:

*fit; fitness; enrol; muscles; pulse; instructor; out of / in shape; breathe; out of breath.*

Ask the students – *How fit are you?* Let them discuss for a few minutes in pairs. Meanwhile, put a cline arrow on the board and ask them to come up and put their names anywhere on the arrow using the board pen:

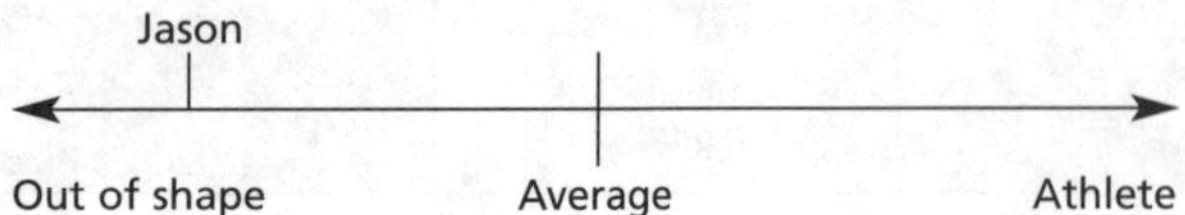


Ask some of the students who put their names on the right why they think they are so fit.

## Role Play instructions

Introduce the role play and tell students that they will now find out how fit they really are. Hand out the cards and give the students 2–3 minutes to read their roles. Tell the fitness instructors not to read through the whole questionnaire now. Remind lower level students that they can ask you about anything they don't understand during the activity. Ask them to use pencil, not pen, to fill in the questionnaires. Encourage them to use the *Target language* expressions. Start the role play when they are ready. Monitor, help with difficult vocabulary and make sure that the instructors ask appropriate questions and that they really get their partners to do the activities (e.g. measure their pulse or touch their toes).

> **Note: How to take your pulse**
> Place the third and fourth finger of your right hand on the inside of your left wrist just below the thumb joint until you feel the pulse. Press firmly and count the beats for 60 seconds using a clock or a watch.

When they have finished, they should rub out the answers on the questionnaire, swap roles and start again.

## Follow-up suggestion

Under the cline arrow you put on the board, you could add another going from 0 – 150 points, on which students can mark their partners' fitness profiles for comparison with their original opinions.

Students could then work in groups of three or four to compile a list of their top five tips for staying in shape. Get feedback at the end.

---

# Enrolling at a gym

Role Plays for Today

## Student A – New gym member

You would like to improve your fitness, so you have just enrolled at the local gym – Wellfit. Today is your first day, and you have to do a fitness test with your fitness instructor. Answer her / his questions honestly, and try to do everything s/he says. Afterwards, s/he will tell you how fit you are. Ask for recommendations at the end about how to start exercising.

> **Target language**
>
> **Talking about habits**
>
> *Usually I…*
> *…drink / smoke / exercise…*
> *…about once / twice / three times a week.*
>
> **Questions to ask**
>
> *Could you repeat the instruction, please?*
> *Like this?*
> *What do you think I should do?*

# Enrolling at a gym

## Student B – Fitness instructor

You work at the Wellfit gym as a fitness instructor. It is your job to test the fitness of all new members of the gym. You must complete the following questionnaire and give them a 'Fitness Profile' when you finish. Don't show the questionnaire to the new member. Think carefully about the correct question to ask, or instructions to give. Use the *Target language* box to help you.

**Complete the questionnaire yourself.**

## General Fitness

**1) Drinking: Units of alcohol each week**
(1 unit = 1 glass of wine, beer or whisky, etc.)

| Units: | ☐ 0 | ☐ 1–3 | ☐ 4–8 | ☐ 9–15 | ☐ over 15 |
|---|---|---|---|---|---|
| Score: | 10 | 8 | 5 | 3 | 0 |

**2) Smoking: Number of cigarettes each week**

| Units: | ☐ 0 | ☐ 1–5 | ☐ 6–10 | ☐ 11–20 | ☐ over 20 |
|---|---|---|---|---|---|
| Score: | 15 | 5 | 3 | 1 | 0 |

**3) Exercising: each week** (write number)

| Units: | ☐ Walking (30 mins) | ☐ Aerobics (30 mins) |
|---|---|---|
| Score: | 5 for each unit | 10 for each unit |

| Units: | ☐ Running / Swimming / Ball Sports (30 mins) |
|---|---|
| Score: | 15 for each unit |

**4) Work: activity type** (tick 1 only)

| Score | Activity |
|---|---|
| 0 | ☐ Sitting down all day (e.g. at a computer) |
| 10 | ☐ Standing up all day (e.g. in a shop) |
| 15 | ☐ Walking all day (e.g. traffic warden) |
| 30 | ☐ Using muscles (e.g. builder) |

## Fitness Test

**Ask the new member to do the following:**

**5) Measure your pulse (heartbeat)**
Before exercise

| Score | Pulse (heartbeats per minute) |
|---|---|
| 20 | ☐ Under 60 |
| 15 | ☐ 60–80 |
| 10 | ☐ 80–100 |
| 5 | ☐ Over 100 |

**6) Try to hold your breath for a minute**

| Score | Result |
|---|---|
| 25 | ☐ Easy |
| 18 | ☐ Successful, but only just |
| 8 | ☐ 40–60 seconds |
| 3 | ☐ Under 40 seconds |

**7) Stand up and try to touch your toes with your legs straight**

| Score | Result |
|---|---|
| 10 | ☐ Can touch the floor |
| 6 | ☐ Can touch the toes |
| 3 | ☐ 5 cm from toes |
| 0 | ☐ 10 cm from toes |

**8) Stand on one leg for a minute with your eyes closed**

| Score | Result |
|---|---|
| 20 | ☐ Easy. S/he didn't even move |
| 10 | ☐ Successful, but nearly lost her / his balance |
| 5 | ☐ 30–60 seconds |
| 0 | ☐ Under 30 seconds |

**9) Put your hands on the side of your chair, and lift yourself up off the chair without touching the ground 3 times for 3 seconds**

| Score | Result |
|---|---|
| 25 | ☐ It was easy. Not even out of breath |
| 18 | ☐ Successful, but breathing heavily |
| 8 | ☐ Only able to do 1–2 lifts |
| 0 | ☐ Not able to do 1 lift |

**10) Measure your pulse again**
After light exercise

| Score | Pulse (heartbeats per minute) |
|---|---|
| 20 | ☐ Under 80 |
| 15 | ☐ 80–100 |
| 10 | ☐ 100–120 |
| 5 | ☐ Over 120 |

## Results

| Score | Fitness Profile |
|---|---|
| Over 150 | **Athlete** Extremely fit. You can exercise every day, but you probably already do. |
| 120–150 | **Sporty** You are very fit, and enjoy exercise. Start exercising 2–3 times a week for one hour and see how you feel. |
| 70–120 | **In shape** You are fit, but you can improve further. Exercise twice a week for 40 minutes for two weeks, and gradually improve. |
| 40–70 | **Average** You have nothing to worry about, but now is the time to start working on your health. Exercise twice a week for 20 minutes, then build up to 40 minutes after three weeks. |
| Under 40 | **Out of shape** You need to start thinking seriously about your health. Try to cut out the bad habits and start with a little gentle exercise: 20 minutes once a week for two weeks, then move up to twice a week. |

### Target language

**Questions and instructions**

*How much / many / often…?*
*What kind of… do you…?*
*Now I'd like you to…*
*Could you… please?*
*What we have to do now is…*

**Results**

*Here's your fitness profile.*
*You are (+ adjective / noun)…*
*You should / shouldn't (+ verb)…*
*I recommend that you (+ verb)…*

 

# 1c Post Office – Teacher's notes

## Time / Level

35–50 minutes / Elementary to Intermediate

## Target language

**Grammar**

Question forms (*Could I...? How many do you want?*)

**Functions**

Making enquiries (*Do you sell...? Is it possible to...?*)

**Vocabulary**

Shopping (*post office, stamps, parcel, scales*)

## Preparation

Copy the main worksheet (one per student or per pair) and the four Customer role play cards below (4 per 8 students). Cut up as indicated.

## Lead–in suggestion

With pre-intermediate or intermediate students, ask them to brainstorm the following question for two minutes: *What things can you do at a post office (in your country)? Write a list. (e.g. post a letter)*

With elementary students, elicit *post office* and go straight into the first exercise on the worksheet.

## Worksheet stages

Hand out the worksheet. Exercise A is a quick vocabulary check, and can be done with the whole class. Exercise B: Do one or two examples and then give students 5–7 minutes to match the remaining customer questions with the appropriate reply.

**Note:** In the UK, 'registered post' is a way to prove that an item has been sent and received. The recipient has to sign for it.

**Answers** 1)d 2)f 3)a 4)g 5)c 6)b 7)h 8)e

Exercise C requires the students to predict how the conversations might continue. First elicit an example from them, then put them into pairs for the rest. You'll probably need to teach the key phrase: *Here you are.* **Note:** 7)h and 8)e would probably not continue.

## Role Play instructions

As far as possible, create (or imagine) a counter in the middle of the classroom. Put half the students behind it (cashiers). Give the other half the role play cards below (Customers A–D). Use some of them more than once if you have over eight students. Put the customers in a queue, and tell the cashiers to call up the customers by saying 'Next please.' Encourage them to use the *Target language* expressions. When they have finished, they should swap roles and start again.

## Follow-up suggestion

Round up by finding out who was the most difficult customer, and who was the most polite cashier.

## Post Office – Customer A

**You need...**

- to send three postcards to your country
- to pay a gas bill
- to change $100 into pounds sterling
- to find out how much a parcel costs to send to your country (don't send it yet!)

## Post Office – Customer C

**You need...**

- to send two parcels to your country (one big, one small)
- to pay a telephone bill
- to change £50 into Euros
- to buy 10 stamps for letters (not international)

## Post Office – Customer B

**You need...**

- to buy an International phone card (£10)
- to buy an envelope
- to send £50 to your country by post
- to send your passport registered post

## Post Office – Customer D

**You need...**

- to phone your country, but you don't have a mobile phone
- to buy 10 postcards
- to send an expensive present by registered post (it cost you £300)
- to send a letter to your parents

 

# Post Office



**A** **What are these things called? Find the words in the customer questions and the replies below. The words are all <u>underlined</u>.**

**B** **Match the customer question to the correct reply.**

## CUSTOMER QUESTION

1) Could I send two <u>postcards</u> to Italy, please?
2) Could I send this <u>parcel</u> to China, please?
3) Could I send this registered post, please?
4) Do you sell international telephone cards?
5) I need to send money by post. What's the best way?
6) Do you sell <u>envelopes</u>? I need A4 size.
7) I need to pay this bill. Can I do it here?
8) Is it possible to exchange money here?

## REPLY

a) Yes. Just fill in this <u>form</u>... That's £4.90, please. Is there anything valuable inside?
b) Yes. They're 55p each. How many do you need?
c) A postal order. You can buy one here. Is it international?
d) Yes. The <u>stamps</u> are 58p each. That's £1.16 please.
e) Yes. But you're in the wrong <u>queue</u>. The Bureau de Change is over there.
f) Of course. Just put it on the <u>scales</u>, please... Do you want to send it airmail?
g) Yes. They cost from £5 to £30. Is it for a mobile phone, or a <u>payphone</u>?
h) Er... No. You need to take it to the bank. There's one on Baker Street, round the corner.

**C** **Look again at the replies. Which ones will continue? What will they say? Tell your partner.**

## Role Play

**Half the students are post office cashiers. Listen to the customers and try to help them.**

**Half the students are customers. The teacher will give you role play cards to read.**

### Target language

**Post office cashier**

*Next please. Can I help you?*
*Where do you want to send it?*
*That's ...(£).* *They cost...(£).*
*Here you are.* *Here's your change.*

**Customer**

*Could I send...(what) (where)?*
*Do you sell...(noun)?*
*I need to... (verb).*
*Is it possible to... (verb)?*
*Sorry. Could you repeat that?*
*Here you are.*

 

# 1d Visiting the Doctor – Teacher's notes

## Time / Level

45–60 minutes / Pre-intermediate to Upper Intermediate

## Target language

**Grammar**

*Should* + verb (*You should get some rest.*)
*Have got* (*I've got a sore throat.*)

**Functions**

Describing how you feel (*I feel hot, and I can't sleep…*)
Asking for and giving advice (*Try not to walk on it for 3 days.*)

**Vocabulary**

Health (*illness, 'flu, hay fever, a runny nose, stress*)

## Preparation

Copy role play cards A and B (one set per pair).
Copy the symptoms and advice table (one per pair).Cut up as indicated.

## Lead-in suggestion

Ask the students:

*What do you do when you are ill?*

Elicit *doctor* (often called *GP* in the UK), *hospital, make an appointment* etc.

*Where does a doctor work?*

Elicit or teach: *surgery / clinic*. Write any useful vocabulary that comes up on the board.
Hand out the symptoms and advice table (one per pair). Instruct the students to try to complete the table with symptoms and advice. Avoid pre-teaching any vocabulary with low level students. The context of the table will make it easier to explain afterwards. Monitor. Go through the answers when they've finished.

**Answers**

**a)** a sore throat **b)** take vitamin C **c)** take paracetamol **d)** diarrhoea **e)** don't eat anything **f)** can't sleep (insomnia) **g)** can't move my hand **h)** go to hospital **i)** a swollen ankle **j)** use crutches **k)** red eyes **l)** prescription medicine

Explain any expressions the students still don't know. Drill any words which are difficult to pronounce (e.g. *diarrhoea, ache*). Tell the students to discuss the questions below the table in pairs. Be sensitive during feedback. Some students may not want to reveal their recent illnesses to the whole class.

## Role Play instructions

Introduce the role play. If much of the vocabulary is new, give them a minute to reread and remember the information in the chart. Hand out the role play sheets. Give the students 3–5 minutes to read through and prepare what they are going to say. Encourage the doctors to work from memory, and to improvise where necessary. Draw their attention to the *Target language*. Start the role play when they are ready. When they have finished, they should swap roles and start again. For more practice, they could change partners and repeat the procedure.

**Extra idea:** You could turn the class into a surgery. Divide it into a waiting room, where all the patients sit, and several consulting rooms, where the doctors receive the patients. The waiting patients can discuss what is wrong with them. This will also enable them to open and close the meeting with the doctor more naturally.

## Follow-up suggestion

Find out briefly who would make a good doctor and why. Did anybody give the wrong diagnosis or advice?

---

# Visiting the Doctor



## Student A – Patient

**You are a patient at your local doctor's surgery. Choose one of the illnesses from the chart and tell the doctor the answers to these questions:**

- How, when and where did it start?
- What symptoms have you got?
- Have you taken any medicine or done anything else to help?

**Student B will try to provide the correct diagnosis. At the end tell student B if s/he was correct about the illness.**

**Target language**

*It started… (a week ago).*
*I feel… (tired, hot, etc.).*
*I had an accident when…*
*It hurts here.*
*I've got… (a sore throat, a swollen ankle).*
*I can't… walk / sleep*
*Is it serious?*
*What should I do?*

# Visiting the Doctor



**Look at the table below. It describes seven common reasons for going to the doctor. Complete the table using the information from the boxes.**

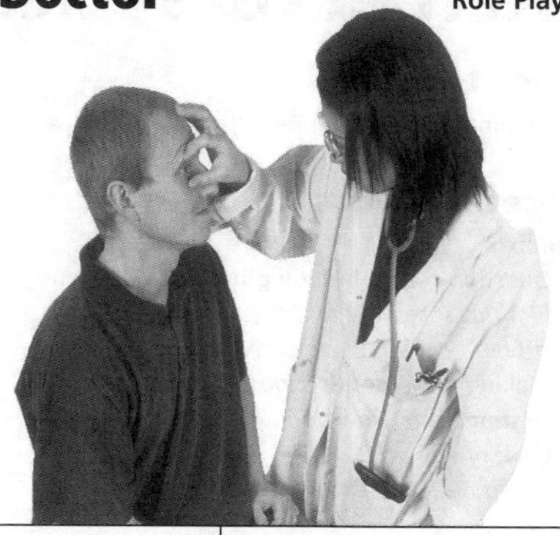

| **Symptoms** | diarrhoea | red eyes |
|---|---|---|
| | a sore throat | can't move my hand |
| | can't sleep (insomnia) | a swollen ankle |

| **Advice** | prescription medicine | take vitamin C |
|---|---|---|
| | go to hospital | use crutches |
| | don't eat anything | take paracetamol |

| Illness/Complaint | Cause | Symptoms | Advice |
|---|---|---|---|
| a cold | a virus, usually caught through contact or sneezing | a runny nose, **a)** ________, a cough | keep warm, get some rest, **b)** ________ |
| the 'flu | a virus, usually caught through contact or sneezing | as for a cold, also a high temperature, aching bones and head | go to bed, **c)** ________ for the temperature and the aches |
| food poisoning | eating food that isn't fresh | stomach ache, vomiting, **d)** ________ | **e)** ________ for 24 hours, get some rest, drink water |
| stress | too many problems, especially at work | **f)** ________, worrying too much, loss of appetite | take sleeping pills, take a long holiday, change your job! |
| a broken arm | a serious fall, (e.g. off a ladder) | a very strong pain in my arm, **g)** ________ | **h)** ________, set arm in plaster |
| a sprained ankle | an unexpected fall, (e.g. when playing football) | **i)** ________, can't walk | bandage the ankle **j)** ________, get plenty of rest |
| hay fever | an allergy to flowers and plants in summer | a runny nose, **k)** ________ | **l)** ________, stay away from parks and gardens |

- Do you agree with all this advice?
- Do you have any other advice for these complaints?
- Which of these complaints have you had over the last year?
- Did you go to the doctor?

---

# Visiting the Doctor

Role Plays for Today

## Student B – Doctor

**You are the doctor. Listen to student A, who will describe her/his symptoms.**

- Ask questions using the *Target language* expressions.
- Tell the patient what you think the illness is.
- Give the patient some advice.

**Try to remember without looking at the chart. At the end, student A will tell you if your diagnosis was correct.**

### Target language

*What seems to be the problem?*
*Does it hurt here?*
*Is the pain getting worse?*
*Do you have... (a cough, a temperature, a swollen ankle)?*
*Can you... (move your hand, go near parks and flowers)?*
*Are you allergic to anything?*
*I think you have...*
*You should / shouldn't...*
*Try (not) to...(verb)*

# 1e Internet café – Teacher's notes

### Time / Level
20–30 minutes / Pre-intermediate to Upper Intermediate

### Target language
**Grammar**

Question forms, including indirect questions (*I'm not sure how to...*)

**Functions**

Making enquiries (*Is it possible to...?*)

Getting help (*How do I...?*)

**Vocabulary**

Computers and the Internet (*scan, transfer*)

### Lead-in suggestion
Put the following questions on the board for discussion in pairs followed by feedback:

*1) What services do Internet cafés provide?*

*2) When did you last use one? What for?*

### Preparation
Copy role play cards A and B (one set per pair). Cut up as indicated.

### Role Play instructions
Pre-teach the following vocabulary if necessary:

*type up; print out; transfer photos; scan*

Put students into A/B pairs and hand out the two role play cards. Give them a few minutes to read their card. Monitor and help with any difficult vocabulary. Let them begin when they're ready. Encourage them to use the *Target language* expressions. Make sure they swap role play cards after they finish Situation 1.

### Follow-up suggestion
Ask the students if they think Internet cafés will become more or less popular in the future and why.

---

## Internet café

Role Plays for Today

### Student A – Customer

**Situation 1**

You are a journalist, and you've just done an interview with an English rock star. Go into the Internet café and find out if you can do the following: You need to type up the interview in Microsoft Word. You need to print out 20 photos from your digital camera (in colour). You then need Broadband Internet access to send the photos and the interview via e-mail to your head office, which is in the USA. You also need a sandwich for lunch, and a receipt.

*(When you've finished, swap role play cards with your partner)*

**Situation 2**

You are a student of English, and have just taken the IELTS exam*. Your university course at Oxford University starts next month. The university has requested some documents. Go into the Internet café and find out if you can do the following: You need to scan your passport and your IELTS exam result certificate into the computer. You need to write a cover letter to send to the university, which you need to print to check for mistakes. You then need Internet access to send the letter, and the scans of your passport and certificate to the university. Find out the total price before you pay.

**Target language**

*Do you have...?*
*Is it possible to... ...here?*
*How much would it cost to...?*
*How do I...?*
*Could I have...?*
*Would it be possible to...?*
*I'm not sure how to...?*
*Which one? This one?*
*That would be really useful.*
*Thanks for your help.*

* *IELTS is a university entrance exam used mainly in the UK and Australia.*

---

## Internet café

Role Plays for Today

### Student B – Assistant

**You work at an Internet café in London. Your partner will come into the café and make enquiries about your services. Here is a list of all the services you provide and costs. Note: All students must show ID.**

| | Standard Price | Student Price |
|---|---|---|
| **Word processing / Office Suite** Microsoft Word®,Excel®, etc. | £1.00 per hour (minimum 30 mins.) | 70p per hour (minimum 30 mins.) |
| **Broadband Internet access** includes use of all e-mail accounts | £1.50 per hour (minimum 30 mins.) | £1.20 per hour (minimum 30 mins.) |
| **Printing** | 10p a sheet (A4) black and white 80p a sheet (A4) colour | |
| **Scanning** | 50p per scan | |
| **Transferring photos from a digital camera** | £3.00 per camera or memory card | |

Café facilities include tea, coffee, soft drinks and a selection of sandwiches and cakes.

**Target language**

*How can I help?*
*Do you need any help using...?*
*Which program do you need?*
*I'll just show you.*
*Sure, we can do that.*
*The price is...*
*It costs more for...*
*Do you have student ID?*
*Do you need a receipt?*

 

# 1f Train station – Teacher's notes

## Time / Level
20–30 minutes / Elementary to Intermediate

## Target language
**Grammar**

Present simple for timetabled future events (*The next train leaves at 07.41.*)

**Functions**

Buying tickets (*How much is a return to…?*)
Making enquiries (*What time does it leave?*)

**Vocabulary**

Train travel and transport (*single, fare, ID,* etc.)

## Lead-in suggestion
Write *train station* on the board and ask the students for vocabulary associated with this place (e.g. *ticket, platform, arrive, delayed*). Build up a list and check the meaning if necessary.

## Preparation
Copy role play cards A and B (one set per pair). Cut up as indicated.

## Role Play instructions
Pre-teach the following vocabulary if necessary: *return; discount; fare; change; ID; departure*
Put students into A/B pairs and hand out the two role play cards. Give them a few minutes to read their card. Make sure they don't show it to their partner. Do a quick demonstration with one student and then let them begin when they're ready. Encourage them to use the *Target language* expressions and to make notes. Make sure they swap over after doing three situations.

## Follow-up suggestion
Ask the students what train travel is like in their country / countries. Is it reliable / fast / cheap / enjoyable? Why? Why not?

✂--------------------------------------------------------------------------------

# Train station

Role Plays for Today

## Student A – Ticket seller

**You work at Brighton train station. Read the information about train prices and times. It is 7.30a.m. and the station is very busy! Try to help your customers.**

**Train fares and times**

| | Single | Return | Next train at... | Journey time |
|---|---|---|---|---|
| **London Victoria** | £8.40 | £10.40 | 07:41 | 52 mins. |
| **Gatwick Airport** | £5.80 | £7.20 | 07:41 | 38 mins. |
| **Heathrow Airport** | £9.80 | £12.00 | 08:11* | 1hr 18 mins. |
| **Canterbury** | £9.40 | £11.80 | 08:11* | 1hr 35 mins. |
| **Dover** | £9.00 | £11.20 | 08:25 | 50 mins. |
| **Eastbourne** | £4.20 | £5.20 | 08:05 | 31 mins. |
| **Worthing** | £3.80 | £4.60 | 08:09 | 26 mins. |

*Change at Gatwick **Note:** All child and student fares are half price.

**Target language**

*Can I help you?*
*Where would you like to go?*
*Single or return?*
*Do you have student ID?*
*That's £10.40, please.*
*The next train leaves at…*
*It takes about … minutes.*
*Don't forget to change at…*

✂--------------------------------------------------------------------------------

# Train station

Role Plays for Today

## Student B – Traveller

**You are at Brighton train station in England. It is 7.30a.m. Choose one of the situations below and go to the ticket office. Each student should do three situations and then change over. Make notes on the prices and train times.**

**A:** Your friend flies into Heathrow Airport this morning at 9.30a.m. You are going to meet her and bring her to Brighton. You have student ID.

**B:** You need to go to London for the day. You are a student but you don't have ID.

**C:** You would like to go to Canterbury or Dover for one day. Find out which is cheapest, and when the next train is. Then decide which city you would like to visit. You are an adult and you are travelling with two children.

**D:** You would like to visit Dover, and return to Brighton today with your three children.

**E:** You are a businessman. Today you need to go to Dover, and tomorrow you need to return to Brighton and then go to London (single). Buy both tickets now.

**F:** You would like to visit either Eastbourne or Worthing today. You only have £5.

**Target language**

*I need to travel to…*
*How much is a single/ return to…?*
*Can I get a student discount?*
*How much is it for children?*
*How long does it take?*
*When does it arrive in…?*
*When does the next train leave?*
*Do I need to change trains?*
*Could you spell that for me, please?*

# 1g Passport Control – Teacher's notes

### Time / Level

45–60 minutes / Elementary to Intermediate

### Target language

**Grammar**

Present continuous and *going to* for future arrangements and plans (*I'm going to study English; Where are you staying?*)

**Functions**

Expressing future arrangements (*Where are you studying?*)

Asking for clarification (*What does ... mean?*)

**Vocabulary**

Education and accommodation (*fees, homestay*)

### Preparation

Copy the immigration officer's questions and the student's answers (one set per pair) and cut up as indicated. Shuffle each set, but do not mix the questions and the answers. Also copy the role play cards below (one set per pair).

### Lead-in suggestion

Elicit *passport control* and ask the students: *Why is it necessary?* Elicit / teach *immigration officer* and elicit some of the questions the immigration officers ask, either in the students' country or in the UK.

Give each pair of students the immigration officer's questions and the student's answers, both sets shuffled up. Tell them to match the questions and the answers. Monitor and check the answers. Then tell them to put the conversation in the most logical order. Lower level students can read out the conversation once in pairs. Ask higher level students to identify the tenses used in the immigration officer's questions to refer to the future, and why they are appropriate (present continuous – future arrangements; *going to* – future intentions / plans).

### Role Play instructions

Ask students to stand up. Divide them into equal groups: A and B. Give out the role play cards. Let them read for 2–3 minutes. Stand the immigration officers (Bs) side by side, and create a queue of the 'students' (As). Officers begin the role play by each shouting: "Next please." They change roles after the first role play and student B becomes a tourist. Make sure student A adapts the questions appropriately.

### Follow-up suggestion

Ask the students which questions were more difficult and why, and whether they gave the best answers. Find out briefly if they all 'passed' passport control successfully!

---

## Passport Control

Role Plays for Today

### Student A

**You are at Passport Control at Heathrow Airport. You have come to the UK to study English. Use your real name and details. Decide:**

- Where are you staying and studying English?
- How long are you here for?
- How will you support yourself?
- What are your future plans?

**When you finish, change roles with student B. You are an immigration officer. Student B is a tourist. Decide which questions to ask. Some will be the same as the example role play, but you will also need to ask about:**

- places to visit
- hotels
- money
- return ticket

**Target language**

**Student**

*Here you are.*
*Here is my passport / ticket.*
*Sorry. Could you speak more slowly?*
*Sorry. I don't understand the question.*
*Could you repeat that please?*
*What does ... mean?*

---

## Passport Control

Role Plays for Today

### Student B

**You are an immigration officer at Heathrow Airport. Interview student A using the questions from the example role play.**

**When you finish, change roles with student A. You are a tourist, not a student. Decide:**

- How long are you here for?
- Which towns / cities are you going to visit and what will you do?
- How much money do you have and what do you plan to buy?
- Which hotel are you staying at?

**Target language**

**Tourist**

*Here you are.*
*Here is my passport / ticket.*
*Sorry. Could you speak more slowly?*
*Sorry. I don't understand the question.*
*Could you repeat that please?*
*What does ... mean?*

 

| Immigration officer's questions | Students' answers |
| --- | --- |
| Good morning. Your passport and landing card, please. | *Good morning. Here you are.* |
| Thank you. How long are you staying in the UK? | *8 months. Until May next year.* |
| Until May. I see. And what is the purpose of your visit? | *I'm going to study English.* |
| Have you studied English before in your country? | *Yes. At school, for about 5 years, and also a little when I was at university.* |
| So why do you need to come here to study English? | *Because I want to learn real English, here in England. Also, my friend said that English schools are very good for conversation practice.* |
| I see. Where are you studying? | *At Oxford House College, in London.* |
| Do you have a letter of invitation? | *Yes, here is the letter. The school fees are paid.* |
| Thank you. That's fine.<br>Where are you staying? | *In homestay accommodation. The school organised it. Here is the address.* |
| Thank you. How are you going to support yourself here in the UK? | *Support? What do you mean?* |
| I mean – how will you pay for your accommodation, food and so on? | *I see. I'm going to open a bank account and transfer some money from Japan.* |
| Do you have evidence of this money? | *Evidence? What does evidence mean?* |
| Evidence means proof… For example, a recent bank account statement. | *Yes. Here you are. From my bank in Japan.* |
| And what are you going to do when your course finishes? | *I'm going back to Japan to get a job, I hope!* |
| Okay. Enjoy your stay in the UK. | *Thank you.* |

# 1h Airport check-in desk – Teacher's notes

## Time / Level

20–40 minutes / Elementary to Intermediate

## Target language

**Grammar**

Various – mixed tenses and question forms

**Functions**

Asking for clarification (*What does ... mean?*)

Explaining difficult words (*'Flammable' means it burns easily.*)

**Vocabulary**

Transport – Plane travel (*take off, aisle, board*)

## Preparation

Copy the main worksheet (one each or one per pair) and the role play card for student A below (one per pair). Cut up as indicated.

## Lead-in suggestion

Write the following on the board:

*a) The plane takes off.*
*b) You wait in the departure lounge.*
*c) You check in your baggage.*
*d) You go through security.*
*e) You board the plane.*

Tell the students to put these in the same order as they always happen, working in pairs. After a minute or two get feedback, and check they understand the vocabulary used (e.g. *board, check-in*).

**Answers** c; d; b; e; a

## Role Play instructions

Introduce the role play, hand out the worksheet and ask them to complete exercise A. Monitor and help where necessary, but avoid explaining all the technical language (*flammable*, etc.) at this stage.

**Answers**
**1** window **2** pack **3** unattended **4** parcels
**5** hand baggage **6** boarding card **7** departure gate

Next the students complete the passenger's lines (B) by writing them underneath the questions to create a dialogue. Note how the passenger doesn't say much, but that the correct answers are nonetheless very important, so comprehension is essential here. When they have finished, check the answers and explain any vocabulary the students are still unsure about.

**Answers**
(in order) Window, please; Yes; Yes; No; No; No; No; What time does the plane take off?; Thank you.

Let lower level students practise reading the conversation from the sheet twice. Now they are ready to do the role play. Give student A in each pair the role play card below. Tell student B to pick up the worksheet. Give the students 2–3 minutes to read their cards. Start the role play when they are ready. Encourage them to use the *Target language* expressions and to improvise freely. When they have finished, they should swap roles and start again. You could encourage strong students to improvise the whole conversation from memory the second time.

## Follow-up suggestion

Put the following questions on the board for students to discuss, followed by feedback:

*Do you enjoy travelling by plane? Why (not)?*
*Where do you prefer to sit? Why?*
*How do you pass the time when you are on a flight? Do you ever get bored?*

---

# Airport check-in desk

Role Plays for Today

## Student A – Passenger

You are a passenger at an airport check-in desk. Listen carefully to student B's questions and give the correct answers. They will be in a different order to the conversation in exercise A. Also, to make it more interesting, ask some of the *Target language* questions. Swap over after you finish.

### Target language

*Sorry. Could you explain what (firearms / flammable / sharp) means?*
*Sorry. Could you repeat the question more slowly, please?*
*Is it possible to get a seat with extra leg room?*
*Could I check in this bag as well, please?*
*Could you be careful with this bag? It's very fragile. ('fragile' means it can break)*
*Is it OK if I take my dog on the plane?*
*Do you know what is for lunch today?*
*How do I get to the departure lounge?*

 

# Airport check-in desk



**A** When you check in for a flight at an airport, they often ask you some very difficult questions. Read the questions below and put one word or expression in each box:

| boarding card | departure gate | parcels | pack | window | hand baggage | unattended |
|---|---|---|---|---|---|---|

Hello. Your ticket and passport please. Thank you... Aisle seat or [1 ________] ?

Is it just the one bag to check in?

Did you [2 ________] your bags yourself?

Any flammable or chemical items, compressed gases or firearms in your baggage?

Have you left your bags [3 ________] at any time since you packed them?

Are you carrying any gifts or [4 ________] on behalf of other people?

And does your [5 ________] contain any of the following items: knives, sharp objects, matches or lighters?

Thank you. Right... Here's your passport and ticket. And here's your [6 ________].
Seat 48A. The [7 ________] is number 14.
Make your way to the departure lounge at least 40 minutes before departure.

13.20. It says just here. But check the information screens in the departure lounge, as this might change.

Enjoy your flight.

**B** Under each of the questions, write what you think the passenger says. Choose from the words and expressions below. You will need to use 'Yes' and 'No' many times.

| Yes. | No. | Thank you. | Window, please. | What time does the plane take off? |
|---|---|---|---|---|

## Role Play

Take it in turns to practise the conversation. Student A – the teacher will give you a role play card. Student B – read the information below.

### Student B – Check-in assistant

Pick up this piece of paper. Don't show it to student A. You are the check-in assistant at an airport. Ask him / her all the questions, but change the order. Be prepared for some difficult questions. Use the *Target language* to answer them. Swap over after you finish.

**Target language**

*_____ means, for example...*
*Sorry. Let me explain...*
*Let me have a look.*
*Yes, we can do that for you.*
*I'm sorry, madam / sir...*
*...we don't allow...*
*...I'm afraid I don't know. Let me ask.*

**Directions**

*Yes. Of course. Just turn left over there and follow the signs.*

# 1i Reporting a crime – Teacher's notes

## Time / Level

30–40 minutes / Pre-intermediate to Upper Intermediate

## Target language

**Grammar**

Asking indirect questions (*Could you tell me…?*)
Past continuous (*I was walking…*)

**Functions**

Describing appearance (*He was quite tall, in his thirties…*)
Expressing degrees of certainty (*I'm not sure.*)

**Vocabulary**

Physical appearance (*in his twenties, long dark hair*)
Clothes (*jeans, T-shirt*)
Crime (*stole, criminal*)

## Preparation

Copy role play cards A and B (one per student), and the thief pictures below (one set per four students – not necessary if you use students in the class as explained below). Cut up as indicated.

## Lead-in suggestion

Put the following questions on the board for discussion in pairs followed by feedback:

1) *What are the most common things that criminals steal in your country?*
2) *Have you ever had anything stolen?*
3) *What should you do if a criminal steals your mobile phone, for example?*

## Role Play instructions

Introduce the role play and hand out the sheets. In pairs, one student gets *Student A – Victim*, the other student gets *B – Police officer*. Give them 2–3 minutes to read their sheets.

**Option 1:** If you think your class would enjoy this, let the victims choose other students in the class to describe to the police officer. Afterwards, you can check how accurate the descriptions were by getting the officers to stand up and 'arrest the criminals'!

**Option 2:** If you feel it would be more appropriate, use the thief pictures below, giving out different pictures to different victims. At the end, you can put all the pictures on the board (enlarge them on a photocopier), and get the officers to 'arrest the criminal' by identifying the appropriate pictures.

**Note:** With both options, make sure the victims keep the identity of the thief a secret.

Once the pairs have finished, get them to change roles. Hand out new copies of the role play sheets.

## Follow-up suggestion

Students create an A4-size 'Wanted' poster for one of their criminals. On it, they draw a picture of the criminal, and write a description of the criminal underneath, and a reward for capture.

# Reporting a crime



## Student A – Victim

**Your mobile phone was stolen by somebody an hour ago. You must decide:**

Where were you when it was stolen?
How did the thief take it?

**Most importantly, you should give the police a detailed description of the thief. Tell them about:**

- approximate age
- height and build (slim or heavy)
- face and hair
- clothes

**When you have finished, ask the police officer to repeat the description to check it is correct.**

**Target language**

**Describing appearance**

*The thief was... in his twenties / quite tall.*
*He / She had... long dark hair / brown eyes.*
*S/he was wearing... an old pair of jeans / a green T-shirt.*

**When you're not sure**

*I can't remember exactly.*
*I'm not sure.*
*I think s/he was...*
*He / She was probably...*

# Reporting a crime



## Student B – Police Officer

**You are a police officer. Student A needs help. Listen to the problem and fill in the stolen item form. Ask any questions you need to get all the information:**

### London Metropolitan Police – Stolen Item Form B738

Name:

Address:

**Description of crime**

What was stolen?

Value (£):

Where was it stolen?

Date of crime:

Time of Day:

What happened?

**Description of thief**

Age:

Height and build:

Face:

Hair:

Clothes:

**Target language**

**Asking indirect questions**

*Could you tell me...*
*Can you explain...*
*Do you know...*

*...what happened exactly?*
*...where you were at the time?*
*...what he looked like?*
*...what time it was?*

# 1j Checking into a hotel – Teacher's notes

## Time / Level
30–45 minutes / Elementary to Intermediate

## Target language
**Grammar**
Question forms (*Does that include breakfast?*)
**Functions**
Making enquiries (*Is the bathroom en suite?*)
**Vocabulary**
Hotels (*double room, en suite bathroom*)

## Preparation
Copy the role play card below (one per pair).

## Lead-in suggestion
Write the following task on the board:

*Think of five questions you need to ask when you check into a hotel.*

Tell the students to work in pairs and give them 4 minutes. Get feedback. Write a list on the board.

## Role Play instructions
Hand out the role play card (one per pair) and read out the first task. Do an example together. Give them 2–4 minutes and then check the answers.

**Answers**
**1** Do **2** Do **3** is **4** Does **5** Is **6** does **7** Is **8** are **9** Are **10** Do **11** Is

Check the students understand *double room* and teach *twin room / single room*. Discuss the two questions underneath the dialogue with them.

**Answers**
It's a small hotel (no credit cards; wife cooks breakfast.) The main problem is all the extra costs that the hotel owner keeps adding!

Tell them to read through the conversation twice in pairs, changing roles after the first reading. Encourage them to work from memory especially at higher levels. Tell the students to practise similar conversations, using the situations given underneath. They should change roles after each one. At the end, get some of the pairs to perform their third conversation in front of the whole class.

## Follow-up suggestion
Find out if any of the students have had similar problems with extra costs when staying at a hotel.

---

# Checking into a hotel

Role Plays for Today

**Read the dialogue and complete the questions with *do, does, is* or *are*.**

| Guest | Hotel owner |
|---|---|
| Hello. 1_______ you speak English? → | A little, yes. |
| 2_______ you have a double room for tonight? | Let me see… Yes, we do. |
| Good. How much 3_______ it? | €40. |
| €40 per person or per room? | Per person. |
| 4_______ that include breakfast? | No. Breakfast is €10 extra, per person. |
| OK. 5_______ the bathroom en suite? | Sorry. What 6_______ 'en suite' mean? |
| It means that it has a private bathroom. | Ah, yes! That's another €10, per person. |
| Right. 7_______ it possible to see the room? | Yes. Come with me. Where 8_______ you from? |
| From England. | Really? 9_______ you on holiday? |
| Yes. With my husband. He's in the car. | Ah, I see. Here is the room. |
| OK. This is fine. Shall I pay now? | Yes, please. That's €130, please. |
| Er… Isn't it €120? | Yes, and €10 for the car park. |
| Right. 10_______ you accept credit cards? | No. Only cash. |
| OK. Here you are. What time's breakfast? | From 8 to 9. My wife gets up early! |
| Oh! 11_______ it possible to have it at 10? | Yes. For an extra €5. |
| Another €5! Per person? | Per person. |
| Oh, all right! Here you are. | And here is your key. Goodnight. |

**Is it a big hotel? What problem does the guest have?**
**Now practise similar conversations, using the information below.**

**Situation 1**
4 guests – mum, dad and 2 children – need 2 rooms for tonight; both en suite. They need dinner tonight and breakfast at 7am tomorrow as they are leaving early.

**Situation 2**
1 guest needs a single room for 3 nights. S/he doesn't like getting up early and doesn't want to pay over €50 per night.

**Situation 3**
Be yourself! You are on holiday with your family or friends.

 

## 1k Complaining in a hotel – Teacher's notes

### Time / Level

20–30 minutes / Pre-intermediate to Advanced

### Target language

**Grammar**

*Will* for spontaneous decisions (*I'll tell them...*)
*There is / there are* (*There aren't any towels.*)

**Functions**

Complaining (*That really isn't good enough!*)
Providing excuses (*We're very busy, sir.*)
Apologising (*I'm terribly sorry, sir / madam.*)

**Vocabulary**

Hotels (*wake-up call, guest, reduction*)

### Preparation

Copy the worksheet and role play cards A and B (one of each per pair). Cut up as indicated.

### Role Play instructions

Hand out the worksheet (one copy per pair) and give them five minutes to do exercise A. As the pairs finish, tell them to discuss the question in exercise B. Get feedback. Write up any other complaints the students thought of on the board. Give them 3–4 minutes to do exercise C and then elicit a possible response to each of the complaints.

Put students into A/B pairs and hand out the two role play cards. Give them a few minutes to read their card. Make sure they don't show it to their partner. Let them begin when they're ready. Encourage them to use the *Target language* expressions. They can swap roles when they finish.

**Idea:** Students may enjoy watching an episode of the *Fawlty Towers* BBC TV series before they do the role play if you can get the recording!

---

# Complaining in a hotel

Role Plays for Today

**A** **Look at this list of complaints in a hotel. Working in pairs, put them in order from the most serious (1) to the least serious (7). Give reasons for your choices.**

- [ ] "There is a party in the room next door. I can't get to sleep."
- [ ] "The TV remote control doesn't work."
- [ ] "I didn't get a wake-up call this morning. I was late for my meeting."
- [ ] "My camera was stolen from the room."
- [ ] "There aren't enough pillows in the room."
- [ ] "There was no hot water left when I took a shower this morning."
- [ ] "The waiter spilt wine all over my dress at dinner last night."

**B** **Which of these problems have you had at a hotel? Can you think of any other problems?**

**C** **Now think of a possible response to each complaint from the receptionist.**
e.g. "I'm so sorry! They're here for a wedding. I'll tell them to keep the noise down."

---

## Student A – Receptionist

You are a receptionist at the Faulty Towers Hotel. It's very busy and lots of guests are complaining. Try to calm them down, explain the problems and be polite. Try not to offer any reductions. If any guests are really angry, take 10% off the price, and offer them free dinner tonight.

**Target language**

*I'm terribly sorry, madam / sir.*
*Oh dear! This has never happened before.*
*I see. What can I do to help?*
*I'm sorry, but reductions are not possible.*
*Can we offer you free dinner tonight?*
*I understand. I'll take 10% off the price.*
*Enjoy the rest of your stay.*

## Student B – Unhappy guest

You are a guest at the Faulty Towers Hotel, but it's been a nightmare since you arrived. You are now very angry. Go down to the reception and complain. Use some of the complaints you studied. Try to get a reduction in the price, or a better room.

**Target language**

*I'm extremely unhappy with...*
*The first problem is...*
*What are you going to do about it?*
*I'm sorry. That really isn't good enough.*
*It's no good making excuses!*
*I demand a reduction!*
*I'm going to report your hotel!*

# 11 Travel Agent – Teacher's notes

## Time / Level

30–45 minutes / Pre-intermediate to Upper intermediate

## Target language

**Grammar**

Question forms (*How far is it from the airport to the hotel?*)

**Functions**

Making enquiries (*Could you tell me about...?*)
Clarifying details (*Is that included in the price?*)

**Vocabulary**

Travel / holidays (*excursion, flight*)
Purchasing (*per person, hire*)

## Preparation

Copy the instruction sheet below (one per pair), the holiday advertisements and the notes for Travel Agent (one set per 3–4 students). Cut up as indicated. Stick the holiday advertisements around the walls of the classroom at the start of the lesson. There should be several copies of each one so that the pairs have plenty to choose from.

## Lead-in suggestion

Pre-teach the following if necessary:
*included in the price; excursion; accommodation; transfer; half-board; bed and breakfast; self-catering; available; hire car.*

Write the following on the board:

*sightseeing holiday*
*beach holiday*
*theme park holiday*

Elicit or explain the difference between the three types of holiday with examples (e.g. *Disneyland*). Tell the students to note down three things you can do on each type of holiday. Get feedback at the end.

## Role Play instructions

Introduce the role play by telling the students that they are in a travel agent's and would like to choose a holiday. Hand out the instruction sheet below (one per pair) and read through A with them. Give them 2–3 minutes to walk around the class and choose their holiday. Then give them 3–5 minutes to think of some questions (and write them down if they need to).

B) Tell them to decide who will play the travel agent and hand out a copy of the appropriate *Notes for Travel Agent* to the appropriate student in each pair. Emphasise to the travel agents that they should not show their cards or offer any information that isn't asked for. Encourage them to use the *Target language*. The role play should take from 4 to 7 minutes.

C) & D) The students repeat the above procedure with a different advertisement taken from the walls of the classroom. As the pairs finish, tell them to look at E, and to prepare to report back to the class on their choice.

## Follow-up suggestion

Each pair tells the whole class which two holidays they found out more about, which one they chose to go on and why. After this, find out from the students if any of them have ever had any problems on holiday caused by 'hidden extras' (i.e. prices or problems that they weren't told about by the travel agent).

---

# Travel Agent



**A** Work in pairs. Look at the holiday advertisements on the walls of the classroom. Choose one holiday that you both like. Think of four to eight questions to ask the travel agent about this holiday. Use the *Target language* for ideas.

**B** One of you should play the role of the travel agent. The teacher will give you more information about the holiday you chose. Read it carefully but ***don't show it to your partner***! Answer their questions but don't give any more information.

**C** Now choose another holiday and think of four to eight questions to ask about this holiday.

**D** The other student will play the role of the second travel agent. As before, don't show the information to your partner, and don't give any information they don't ask for!

**E** Now together, decide which of the two holidays you would like to go on and why. Tell the other students about your decision.

**Target language**

*Is... ...included in the price?*
*How far is it from... to...?*
*Could you tell me more about...*
*the hotel?*
*For example...*
*how many meals do we get?*
*how many stars does the hotel have?*
*What else do I have to pay for?*
*What about...*
*the excursions?*
*the hire car?*
*the transfer?*
*Do you have any photos?*
*Thanks for your help.*

 

## Costa del Sol, Spain

**ONLY £145 (7 days) or £205 (14 days)**

★ hotel near the sea

★ flights and hotel included in price

★ excursions available

## Rome and Naples, Italy

**ONLY £165 (7 days)**

★ luxury tour bus

★ bed and breakfast hotel accommodation included in price

★ city guide

## Trinidad, Caribbean

**ONLY £340 (14 days)**

★ self-catering beachfront hotel

★ direct flight and transfer included in price

★ scuba diving and windsurfing

## Florida, USA

**ONLY £380 (10 days)**

★ visit Miami or Disney World

★ flights, half-board hotel and hire car included in the price

★ available all year round

## Costa del Sol, Spain

**Notes for Travel Agent**

**£145 (7 days) or £205 (14 days)**

1) 3-star hotel is 10 kilometres from the sea. Free minibus every 30 minutes.
2) Flights are included in the price, but transfer from the airport is an extra £35 per person.
3) 2-star hotel. Breakfast is included in the price, but not lunch or evening meals.
4) Excursions are available for £55 per person:
   a) visit to a vineyard (wine farm)
   b) visit to Barcelona
   c) fishing boat trip on the sea
5) This price only available from September to April.

## Rome and Naples, Italy

**Notes for Travel Agent**

**£165 (7 days)**

1) Luxury tour bus departs from Rome.
2) Price does not include the flight to Rome.
3) 2-star hotels are not in the city centre.
4) 3 days in Rome, 3 days in Naples and 1 day travelling between the two cities.
5) City guide only for 1 day in Rome and 1 day in Naples. The guide speaks intermediate English, and excellent Italian.
6) This price is only available in November, January and February.
7) No excursions are included in the price.

## Trinidad, Caribbean

**Notes for Travel Agent**

**£340 (14 days)**

1) Self-catering accommodation means that the guests have to cook for themselves. All apartments include kitchen, lounge, bedroom and bathroom.
2) Direct flight is only available on Wednesday. Saturday flight is via Miami (2 hours longer).
3) Beachfront hotel (2-star) is in the middle of a town.
4) Scuba diving and windsurfing equipment costs £10 per day to hire.
5) Transfer from the airport is by bus, every 30 minutes.
6) This price is for July to October (rainy season).

## Florida, USA

**Notes for Travel Agent**

**£380 (10 days)**

1) Price is for Miami or Disney World, not both.
2) All flights go to Miami.
3) Hire car is free, but insurance costs $280 per car for 10 days.
4) Price does not include entry into Disney World ($520 extra per person for a 10-day visit).
5) Miami hotel (3-star) is in city centre, 3 kilometres from the beach. Disney World Hotel (3-star) is a 10-minute walk from the resort.
6) Hotel price includes breakfast and evening meal.
7) You must organise and pay for your own visa.

 

# 2a Supermarket shopping – Teacher's notes

## Time / Level

30–45 minutes / Elementary to Intermediate

## Target language

**Grammar**

Countable and uncountable nouns (*There aren't any plastic bags.*)

**Functions**

Enquiring about products (*Do you have any fresh tomatoes?*)

**Vocabulary**

Food (*fresh fish, bananas, eggs*)
Shopping (*checkout, sold out, receipt*)

## Preparation

Copy the main worksheet (one per student).

## Lead-in suggestion

Put the following questions on the board for discussion in pairs followed by feedback:

1) *Do you like shopping in supermarkets? Why (not)?*
2) *Does everybody shop in supermarkets in your country?*
3) *Where else can you buy food?*
4) *What did you buy last time you went shopping for food? How much did it cost?*

## Role Play instructions

Hand out the worksheet, one per student.

A) Get students to complete exercise A by drawing arrows. At least one logical answer is given for each customer question in the same section on both lists.

B) Tell the students that all the words in the box are from the questions or answers. Give them three minutes to explain any that they know to their partner. When they have finished, get feedback and explain any words the students don't know. Drill the pronunciation of 'aisle'.

C) Show them how to fold their piece of paper so that each student can only see either Customer or Store assistant. Let them practise asking and answering questions for 3–5 minutes depending on the level. Make sure they swap over and do both roles.

D) Divide the class equally into assistants and customers. Tell the customers to take the worksheets, and get them all to stand up for a mingle activity. The customers should choose questions in random order to ask the assistant – one question to each. The assistants should try to remember or improvise an answer. You could choose one (or two) of the assistants to be on the checkout – create a little sign, saying 'checkout' and ask the student to sit down at a desk near the door. Encourage them to act it out and to extend the speaking turns by participating yourself. After five minutes, they all swap roles. This time, the customers should change the underlined words in the questions for suitable alternatives. Elicit a few examples to ensure they understand.

## Follow-up suggestion

Play the alphabet memory game. Start like this:

*"I went to the supermarket and I bought… an apple."*

The next student must repeat this and add a supermarket item beginning with 'b' (*some biscuits*). The game continues with each student adding another item all through the alphabet. Omit Q, X, Z. Do the last one as a whole group.

 

# Supermarket shopping

**A** **Read the customer's questions and match them with the assistant's answers.**

*Fold here*

### Target language – Customer

**Finding your way about**

*Excuse me…*

*Do you have any trolleys / baskets?*
*Where can I find fresh vegetables?*
*Do you have a frozen fish section?*

**Asking about products**

*Do you have any fresh tomatoes?*
*Why isn't there any toothpaste here?*

**Asking for help**

*Could you recommend a good red wine?*
*What's the difference between these two types of coffee?*
*Which is the best washing powder for everyday use?*

**At the checkout**

*Could I pay here? I've only got 3 items.*
*Could you check the price on this?*
*Is this 'buy one, get one free'?*

**Paying**

*How much is that?*
*Can I pay by credit card / cash / cheque?*
*I think there's a mistake on the receipt.*

**After paying**

*Where's the nearest bus stop?*
*How can I apply for a storecard?*
*Do you have a toilet in the store?*

### Target language – Store assistant

**Finding your way about**

*They're in aisle 12, next to the fresh fruit.*
*Yes. It's over there. Can you see?*
*They're by the entrance.*

**Asking about products**

*I'm sorry. We've sold out.*
*I'm not sure. I'll have a look in the storeroom.*

**Asking for help**

*Try the supermarket brand. It washes very well.*
*What about this one? It's on special offer.*
*This one is much stronger, for espresso.*

**At the checkout**

*Yes. But this till is cash only.*
*Yes. The second one is free.*
*Yes, of course. It's £1.15.*

**Paying**

*Is there? Let me see.*
*Yes, of course.*
*That's £43.52, please.*

**After paying**

*Yes. It's by the entrance.*
*Just across the street, opposite the store.*
*Fill in this form and bring it back next time you are here.*

**B** **Useful vocabulary**

**Can you explain these words and expressions to your partner?**

trolley  basket  aisle  storecard  sell out  till
frozen  fresh  special offer  buy one, get one free

**Check the answers with your teacher.**

**C** **Practise in pairs**

**Fold your piece of paper along the line. One student is the customer. One student is the store assistant. The customer should ask questions. The store assistant should give the answer. Swap over after a few minutes.**

**D** **Role Play**

**Everybody stand up. The teacher will divide you into customers and store assistants.**

**Customers**
You can look at your piece of paper. Ask one of the questions to each of the store assistants. Listen to their answer, and correct their mistakes.

**Store assistants**
You can't look at your piece of paper. Try to remember the correct answer to the customers' questions.

**Swap over after 5 minutes. This time, the customers should change the underlined words in the questions:**
"Where can I find ~~fresh vegetables~~ fruit juice?"

# 2b Clothes shop – Teacher's notes

### Time / Level

45–60 minutes / Elementary to Intermediate

### Target language

**Grammar**

Demonstratives (*Oh, those are nice.*)

**Functions**

Expressing personal preferences (*I don't like that colour.*)

Paying compliments (*They suit you!*)

**Vocabulary**

Clothes (*jeans, shirt, top*)

Shopping (*try on, just looking, look great*)

### Preparation

Copy the worksheet (one per pair) and the 3 customer role play cards below (one set per 6 students). Cut up as indicated.

### Lead-in suggestion

Tell the students to discuss the following questions in pairs followed by feedback:

*1) Do you enjoy shopping for clothes? Why (not)?*
*2) What clothes do you need to buy? Why?*
*3) What was the last thing you bought?*

### Role Play instructions

Introduce the role play and hand out the worksheet.

A) Give the students 5 minutes to complete the conversation. Check the answers.

**Answers**
**1** just looking **2** colour **3** size **4** will suit **5** try them on **6** tops **7** a medium **8** go with **9** doesn't fit

Check students understand the meaning of *suit* (v); *go with; fit; try on; top.*

B) First students read the conversation out in pairs. Then the assistant should pick up the copy, so that the customer can't see and must perform their role from memory. Demonstrate if necessary. They can prompt their partner when necessary. Make sure both students have time to play the role of customer from memory before you move on to the whole class role play.

**Idea:** If you have time, to practise singular to plural transformations, you could now get them to change 'jeans' for 'shirt' in the conversation, and to change all the demonstratives and pronouns to agree with a singular noun (*these* → *this; they* → *it;* etc.).

C) Divide the class into assistants and customers. Tell the assistants to keep the worksheet. Give the customers one of the three role play cards below. Give them 2–3 minutes to read and to try to remember the sentences they must use. Start the role play when they are ready. When they have finished, they can swap roles and start again.

### Follow-up suggestion

Find out if they all managed to use their expressions. Then put the students into groups of three to tell each other about their favourite item of clothing. Put these prompts on the board to give them ideas for questions:

*When? Where? How much? Why I like?*
*How often I wear? What I go with?*

Before they begin, get them to ask you the questions, and give your answers as a model. Then let them ask each other. Get feedback at the end.

---

### Customer A

You are a customer in a clothes shop. You would like to buy **some jeans**. During the role play you <u>must</u> say:

**1)** I don't like that colour!

**2)** Can I try them on?

**3)** They don't fit me.

**You can say them in any order. Try to remember them without looking at this card.**

### Customer B

You are a customer in a clothes shop. You would like to buy **a coat**. During the role play you <u>must</u> say:

**1)** I'm looking for a coat.

**2)** That one's too expensive.

**3)** It goes with my bag.

**You can say them in any order. Try to remember them without looking at this card.**

### Customer C

You are a customer in a clothes shop. You would like to buy **a shirt**. During the role play you <u>must</u> say:

**1)** That's the wrong size.

**2)** I like your shirt!

**3)** Where's the fitting room?

**You can say them in any order. Try to remember them without looking at this card.**

 

# Clothes shop



**A** Put one of the words from the box into each gap in the conversation:

| | | | |
|---|---|---|---|
| **VERBS:** | doesn't fit | just looking | |
| | try them on | go with | will suit |
| **NOUNS:** | colour | tops | a medium size |

## Conversation in a clothes shop

**Assistant:** Are you all right?

**Customer:** Yeah, fine. I'm 1 ______________ at the jeans. Are these all you have?

**Assistant:** No. We have some more over here. What 2 ______________ are you after?

**Customer:** Blue or grey.

**Assistant:** And what 3 ______________ are you?

**Customer:** 32.

**Assistant:** We have these ones.

**Customer:** Oh, those are nice. How much are they?

**Assistant:** They're £59.95.

**Customer:** Do you have anything cheaper?

**Assistant:** What about these ones? They're black, but I think they 4 ______________ you.

**Customer:** How much are they?

**Assistant:** £39.95.

**Customer:** That's OK. Where can I 5 ______________ ?

**Assistant:** The fitting rooms are just over there.

**Customer:** Thanks... Oh! These 6 ______________ are nice – and only £5.95 each. Do you have 7 ______________ ?

**Assistant:** Yeah. Here you are.

(3 MINUTES LATER)

**Assistant:** How were they?

**Customer:** Yeah, they were fine. Very comfortable, and they 8 ______________ these shoes.

**Assistant:** Yes, they do. How was the top?

**Customer:** Not so good. It 9 ______________ . I'll just take the jeans.

**B Practise in pairs**

Now read the conversation with another student. Read it once and remember the important details. Then the customer can try to do it without looking. Play both roles – Shop assistant and Customer.

**C Whole class Role Play**

The teacher will divide the class into customers and shop assistants. The teacher will give the customers a role play card. The shop assistants should read this information:

## Shop assistant

You are an assistant in a clothes shop. Try to help the customers. During the role play, try to use these sentences. Tick them (✓) when you use them:

- ☐ They really suit you! / It really suits you!
- ☐ Try a different colour.
- ☐ What size are you?
- ☐ It goes / They go with your shoes.
- ☐ What colours do you like?
- ☐ You look great!
- ☐ Why don't you try it / them on?

 

# 2c DIY shop – Teacher's notes

## Time / Level

30–40 minutes / Pre-intermediate to Upper intermediate

## Target language

**Grammar**

Preposition + gerund (*…for opening bottles.*)
Verb patterns (*It helps you dig holes.*)

**Functions**

Paraphrasing / Describing an object without its name (*You use it for pouring water into a bottle.*)
Negotiating a solution (*Have you got something a bit smaller?*)

**Vocabulary**

Shapes and materials (*round, plastic*)
DIY (*pliers, funnel, padlock*)

## Preparation

Copy role play sheets A and B (one set per pair) and the hardware items for Student A's shop and Student B's shop (one set of both per pair). Cut up as indicated.

## Lead-in suggestion

Act out the following (or similar) situation: Pretend you've lost something, and start looking round for it. The students should become interested. Say something like: *I've lost my…er… I've forgotten what it's called. It's long, made of metal and nylon. It's black and silver and it's for keeping you dry in the rain.* Students should come up with 'umbrella'. Tell them that what you just did is a very common, natural feature of spoken language (paraphrasing) when we don't know or can't remember the word for something. Elicit from the students the sentences you used to paraphrase 'umbrella' and write them on the board. Tell students to try paraphrasing the following in pairs:

*corkscrew*    *headphones*    *batteries*    *comb*

(You can draw pictures if necessary). Get feedback. Elicit kinds of shop where paraphrasing might be quite common (even for native speakers). *DIY shop* or similar should come up.

## Role Play instructions

Split the class into two halves – customers (A) and shop assistants (B). Give out the respective role play sheets and give them a few minutes to read Part 1. If possible, rearrange the room to create a long counter, and a table behind it where the assistants can put their items. This should be far enough away so that the customers can't see the items. Stand the assistants behind the counter and give each one a set of the cut up items for student B's shop. They should spread them out on the back table. Emphasise that they should try to sell the most expensive items to the customers. Start the role play when they are all ready by having the customers come into the shop. Monitor carefully to ensure that neither customers nor assistants start showing the images of the items, but that they use language to explain what they need. When most of the customers have finished, find out if they got what they needed for their £20. They can then move onto Part 2, which requires them to swap roles and start again. Don't forget to give the As the other set of hardware items.

## Follow-up suggestion

Students may be interested to learn the correct names and pronunciation for the objects they paraphrased in the role play. Write the following words on the board:

*trowel*    *pliers*    *dustpan (and brush)*    *plug socket*
*wrench*    *plug*    *funnel*    *hole punch*    *padlock*
*tool box*    *nuts and bolts*    *plunger*

Drill pronunciation of each, and ask students to show the appropriate image on their role play sheets. If time, elicit the function of each.

# DIY (Do it yourself) shop

## Describing an object without its name

## Student A

**Part 1**

**You are a customer in a DIY shop. You need the following things, but you don't know their names in English. Describe them to the assistant, say what they are for and see if they bring you the correct object. Don't forget to check the price of each, and ask for cheaper options if necessary. You have £20.00 to spend.**

**Item 1**
– for general repairs

**Item 2**
– You need about 10
(different shapes and sizes)

**Item 3**
(size: about 10–15cm)

**Item 4**
– for the door to your garage

**Item 5**
– for European electrical equipment

**Item 6**
(size: small 10–20cm)

**Part 2**

**You work in a DIY shop. The teacher will give you the things you have for sale. Don't let the customers see them. Here comes your first customer. Try to sell her / him the most expensive item in each range.**

**Note: Minimum purchase on credit cards: £30.00.**

### Target language

**Describing size and shape**

*It's... square.*
*round.*
*long.*
*flat.*

*It's made of... metal.*
*plastic.*
*wood and rubber.*

*It's about this big. (show)*
*It's the same size as a... (+ noun)*
*They are usually white / silver.*

**Describing function**

*You use it for... repairing leaks.*
*opening bottles.*

*It helps you (to)... dig holes.*
*pour water.*

*It stops you from... losing your tools.*
*making mistakes.*

*You use it with a... hammer.*
*bottle.*

**Negotiating**

*Have you got anything smaller / stronger?*
*I don't need so many.*
*That's... the wrong type.*
*a bit expensive.*

# DIY (Do it yourself) shop

## Describing an object without its name

## Student B

**Part 1**

You work in a DIY shop. The teacher will give you the things you have for sale. Don't let the customers see them. Here comes your first customer. Try to sell her / him the most expensive item in each range.

**Part 2**

You are a customer in a DIY shop. You need the following things, but you don't know their names in English. Describe them to the assistant, say what they are for and see if they bring you the correct object. Don't forget to check the price of each and get them as cheaply as possible.

**You only have a credit card to pay with.**

**Item 1** – for cleaning

**Item 2** – for paper

**Item 3** – just the box (size: about 50–75cm)

**Item 4** – for the bath

**Item 5** – for gardening

**Item 6** (size: small 20cm)

### Target language

**Describing size and shape**

*It's… square.*
*round.*
*long.*
*flat.*

*It's made of… metal.*
*plastic.*
*wood and rubber.*

*It's about this big. (show)*
*It's the same size as a… (+ noun)*
*They are usually white / silver.*

**Describing function**

*You use it for… repairing leaks.*
*opening bottles.*

*It helps you (to)… dig holes.*
*pour water.*

*It stops you from… losing your tools.*
*making mistakes.*

*You use it with a… hammer.*
*bottle.*

**Negotiating**

*Have you got anything smaller / stronger?*
*I don't need so many.*
*That's… the wrong type.*
*a bit expensive.*

 

## Items for Student A's shop

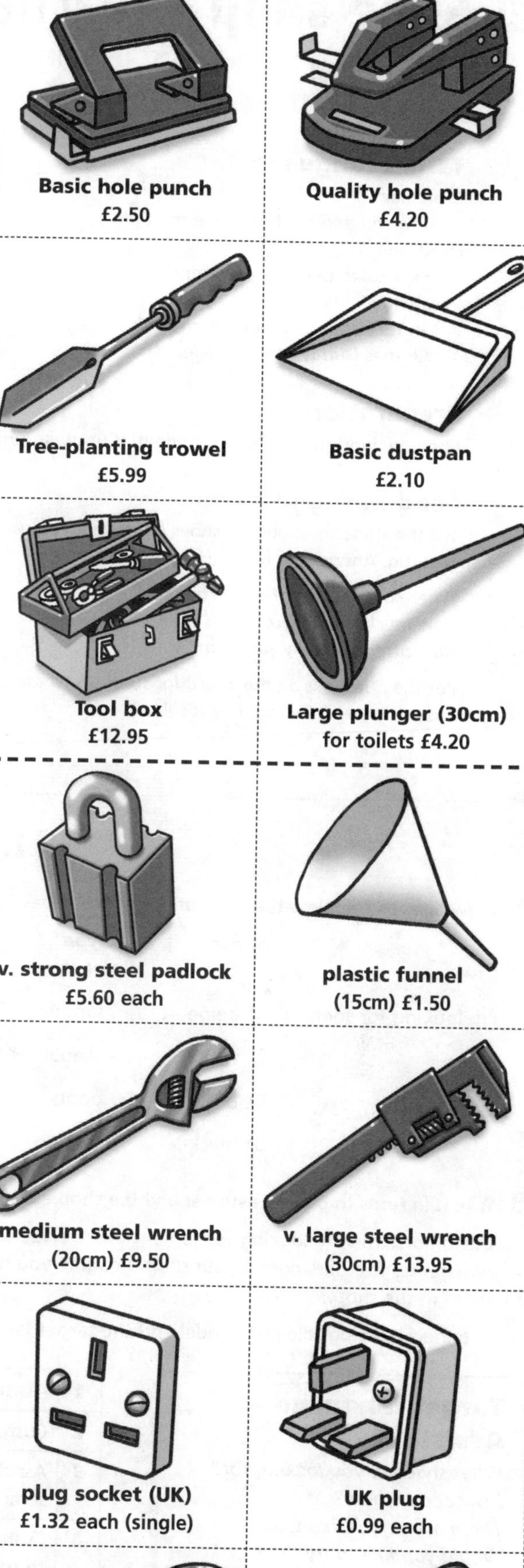

**Plastic plug**
£0.90

**Fun plug**
£3.00

**Basic hole punch**
£2.50

**Quality hole punch**
£4.20

**Bricklayer's trowel**
£8.99 (left-handed)

**Garden trowel**
£4.99

**Tree-planting trowel**
£5.99

**Basic dustpan**
£2.10

**Quality dustpan**
£3.60

**20 piece tool kit**
£22.74

**Tool box**
£12.95

**Large plunger (30cm)**
for toilets £4.20

**Small plunger (20cm)**
for sinks £3.50

## Items for Student B's shop

**steel padlock**
£2.50 each

**v. strong steel padlock**
£5.60 each

**plastic funnel**
(15cm) £1.50

**steel kitchen funnel**
(15cm) £3.50

**small steel wrench**
(10 cm) £4.99

**medium steel wrench**
(20cm) £9.50

**v. large steel wrench**
(30cm) £13.95

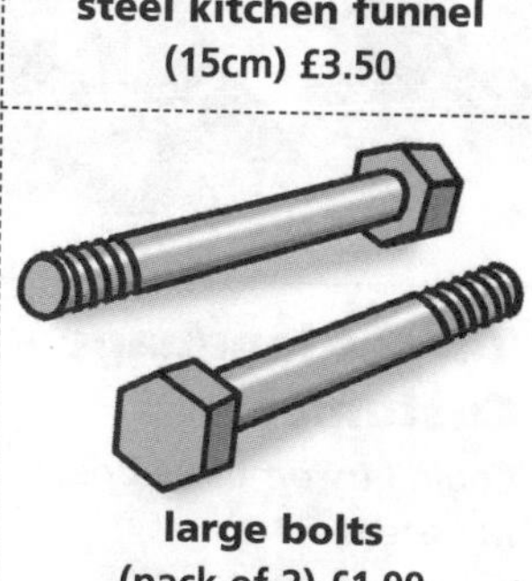

**large bolts**
(pack of 2) £1.99

**nuts and bolts**
(pack of 20) £4.50

**plug socket (UK)**
£1.32 each (single)

**UK plug**
£0.99 each

**plug socket (European)**
£2.50 each (double)

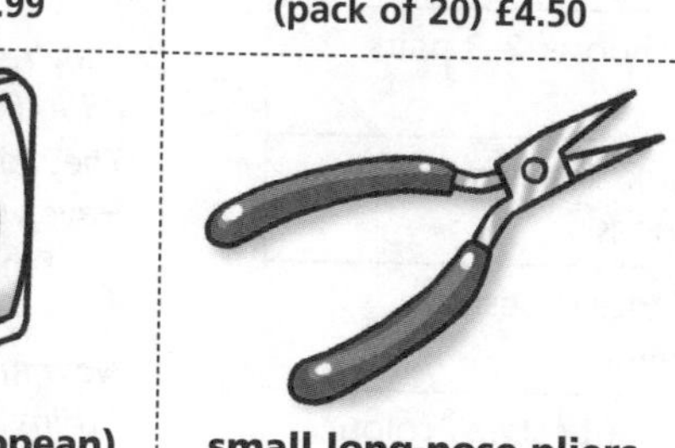

**small long-nose pliers**
£3.59

**large bolt pliers**
£4.50

**all purpose pliers**
£3.99

# 2d Shoe shop – Teacher's notes

## Time / Level

25–40 minutes / Elementary to Intermediate

## Target language

**Grammar**

*Too* and *enough* (*These are too tight.*)

**Functions**

Expressing personal preferences (*I don't like the colour.*)

**Vocabulary**

Shoes (*sandals, slip-ons, high heels*)
Clothes (*suit* (v), *try on, style*)

## Preparation

Copy the worksheet (one per student). Cut up as indicated.

## Lead-in suggestion

Tell the students about the shoes / footwear you're wearing. Answer the following questions:

*Where did you buy them? When?*
*How much did they cost?*
*How often do you wear them?*

Put the questions on the board for students to ask and answer in pairs, followed by feedback.

## Role Play instructions

A) Hand out the worksheet, one per student, and tell them to complete the descriptions of the pictures.

> **Answers**
> **B)** white trainers with laces **C)** brown slip-ons for work
> **D)** black boots with high heels.

Use the pictures to check the vocabulary in the descriptions (e.g. *buckles, slip-ons,* etc.).

B) Read through the role play instruction with them and check the *Target language*. Do a demonstration yourself (as assistant) with a strong student (customer). Include plenty of mime (picking up a shoe, fitting it on the foot). Then send the customers out of the 'shop'. The role play begins when the customers enter the shop. When they've finished, swap them over and repeat the process.

**Idea:** If the floor isn't too dirty, you could get the customers to take off their shoes and give them to the assistants before they leave the shop. This makes for a much more realistic role-play! Alternatively, use photos cut up from a catalogue.

✂ - - - - - - - - - - - - - - - - - - - - - - - - - - - - - - - -

# Shoe shop

Role Plays for Today

**A Draw lines to complete the descriptions of the shoes in the pictures:**

| | *colour* | *type of shoe* | *extra information* |
|---|---|---|---|
| I'm looking for some… | A) beige | slip-ons | with buckles. |
| | B) white | sandals | with high heels. |
| | C) brown | boots | with laces. |
| | D) black | trainers | for work. |

**B Take it in turns to be the customer and the shop assistant.**

**Customers:** You are looking for some shoes. Decide which style and colour.
**Assistants:** The classroom is your shop. Imagine you have lots of different styles in the shop.

Use the following role play model and the target language expressions:

### Target language – Assistant

*What style are you looking for?*
*How about these?*
*These are very fashionable.*
*Would you like to try them on?*
*What size are you?*
*Here you are.*
*How do they feel?*
*They really suit you!*
*Maybe you need a different size?*
*Those ones cost £55.*

| | |
|---|---|
| 1 | Assistant greets customer |
| 2 | Customer says what s/he wants |
| 3 | Assistant shows customer some shoes |
| 4 | Customer chooses 2–3 pairs to try on |
| 5 | Assistant asks for size and gets the shoes |
| 6 | Customer tries shoes on, makes comments |
| 7 | They discuss fit / style / colour |
| 8 | Customer makes a decision |

### Target language – Customer

*Could I try on those ones?*
*My size is...*
*They're (a bit) too tight.*
*They're not big enough.*
*I don't like the colour.*
*They're very comfortable.*
*Have you got…*
*…the next size up / down?*
*…something a bit cheaper?*
*How much are they?*
*I think I'll take them.*
*I think I'll leave it.*

 

# 2e Traditional restaurant – Teacher's notes

## Time / Level

30–60 minutes / Pre-intermediate to Upper intermediate

## Target language

**Grammar**

*Will* for placing orders (*I'll have...*)
Indirect and direct question forms (*Could you tell me...? Would you like...?*)

**Functions**

Enquiring about dishes (*Could you tell me what ... is?*)
Complimenting food (*This is delicious!*)
Complaining (*This soup is cold.*)

**Vocabulary**

Food (*peppers, stewed, pudding, prawns*)

## Preparation

Copy the role play cards. For every 3–6 customers, you'll need at least one waiter. Copy the menu (one per pair). Cut up as indicated. Copy the restaurant language activity below (one per pair; optional).

## Lead-in suggestion

Put the following questions on the board for discussion in pairs followed by feedback:

*When did you last visit a restaurant? Who with? What did you have? What was the meal like?*

## Optional: Restaurant language

Hand out the activity (one per pair) and read instruction A with the students. Give them 3 minutes to do it in pairs, then check the answers. Next ask them to do exercise B, also working in pairs, and check the answers again.

> **Answers**
> **A 1)** C-W **2)** W-C **3)** C-C **4)** C-W **5)** C-C **6)** C-W **7)** C-C **8)** C-W **9)** C-C **10)** W-C
> **B** Most likely order: 10; 3; 9; 1; 6; 7; 4; 2; 8; 5 (9 could be before or during the order)

If time, get feedback to the board for the possible replies. This language will be useful during the role play.

## Role Play instructions

Divide the class into waiters and customers (depending on student numbers, you can put 3–6 customers at each table, and have one waiter per table). Hand out the role play cards and give the students 2–3 minutes to read them. Tell the customers that they have all got different characters, and that they should keep them secret. Check that they all understand that they have to guess each others' characters. When they're ready to start, give the waiters the menus and send the customers out of the room for a moment. Tell the waiters to organise the chairs into a restaurant-like environment and put on some background music. The role play begins when the waiters 'open the restaurant' and greet the customers as they walk in. Times for the role play itself will vary from 12–25 minutes, depending on the students! Avoid explaining difficult vocabulary on the menu until after the role play (more realistic).

## Follow-up suggestion

Write the following on the board:

*Who was...*
*1) complaining 2) enthusiastic 3) worried*
*4) talkative 5) mean 6) inexperienced?*

Get feedback, first from the waiters, and then the other customers. It should be easy to guess.

> **Answers 1)** B **2)** A **3)** D **4)** C **5)** E **6)** F

Students may also have some questions about the vocabulary on the menu.

---

# Traditional restaurant

Role Plays for Today

**A Look at the comments below. Who is speaking? Who to?**
**Write: C → W (*customer to waiter*), W → C or C → C**

1) Sorry. Could you explain what this is, please? ☐
2) Would you like to see the dessert menu? ☐
3) Let's get something to drink while we're deciding. ☐
4) Excuse me. This steak is rare. I asked for medium. ☐
5) How much shall I leave for the tip? ☐
6) I'll have the salmon, please. ☐
7) The soup's delicious. How's the salad? ☐
8) Could we have the bill, please? ☐
9) What are you going to have, dear? ☐
10) Will this table be all right for you? ☐

**B Now put them in the most likely order. Which is first, second... last? Also, think of a possible reply for each statement.**

# Bragg's Traditional English Restaurant

since 1749

# Menu

## Starters

*All starters are £4.25. Fresh bread rolls and butter are included.*

**Grilled Rice and Tuna Peppers**
Half a red and a yellow pepper with a delicious tuna filling

**Caesar Salad**
A light, low-fat salad with bacon and parmesan

**Cornish Omelette**
Made with wild mushrooms and cheddar cheese

**Tomato and Basil Soup**
Fresh tomatoes, roasted with fresh basil in a creamy soup

## Main Courses

*All main courses are £9.80 unless otherwise stated.*
*Served with any of the following accompaniments: vegetables; side salad; chips; new potatoes*

**Steak, Guinness and Mushroom Pie**
Chunks of steak in a Guinness and mushroom sauce inside a pastry casing

**Cod and Chips in a Tartare Sauce**
Fresh cod in batter and deep fried, served with tartare sauce and chips

**Roast Beef and Yorkshire Pudding**
Organic beef served with roasted red onion, vegetables and Yorkshire pudding

**Honey Glazed Roast Chicken £10.95**
Half a slow-roast chicken served with an apple and walnut stuffing

**Prawn and Salmon Fish Cakes on a bed of Rice**
Prawns and salmon mixed with mashed potato, onion and parsley

**8oz Organic Fillet Steak £12.50**
Scottish beef, cooked to your choice and served with caramelised onions

## Puddings and Desserts

*All puddings are just £3.50. All served with cream, ice-cream or custard. Go on, treat yourself!*

**Spotted Dick**
Traditional sponge pudding with raisins

**Chocolate Chip Pudding**
Chocolate sponge with chocolate chips – for convicted chocaholics!

**Apple Crumble**
Stewed apples with an oat crumble topping

**Homemade Devon Ice Cream**
Homemade ice cream, available in vanilla, strawberry, chocolate or toffee

## Drinks

*Red Wines*

**Cabernet Sauvignon, Chile**
£14.95 Bottle £3.95 Glass

**Cotes du Rhone, France**
£13.95 Bottle £3.85 Glass

**Barbera, Italy**
£13.95 Bottle £3.85 Glass

*White Wines*

**Sauvignon Blanc, France**
£11.95 Bottle £3.40 Glass

**Pinot Grigio, Italy**
£14.95 Bottle £3.95 Glass

**Champagne, France**
£36.95 Bottle

*Other Drinks*

**Mineral Water**
£3.95 Bottle £1.25 Glass

**Cola, Lemonade, Orange Juice**
£1.25

**Beers – Holsten Pils, Stella Artois, Corona – £3.80**

**Tea and Coffee (espresso, cappuccino or filter) £1.80**

*Customers may leave tips at their discretion. Any comments or complaints, please ask for the manager.*

### Target language

**Customer**

*Could you tell me…*
*…what this means?*
*…if you have any…*
*…fish dishes?*
*…French wine?*
*I'll have the (soup) for starters and the (steak) for the main course, please.*
*Can I have my steak…*
*…rare / medium / well-done?*
*The (roast beef) is fantastic!*
*That was delicious, thank you.*

 

# Traditional restaurant



## Waiter

**You are a waiter at Bragg's English Restaurant. You must be patient, polite and punctual at all times. Follow this order for the role play:**

**1)** Show the customer to the table, give the menu and take orders for drinks.

**2)** Return with the drinks, serve the wine and take orders for starters and main course (ask: "What accompaniments would you like with your main course?")

**3)** Bring the starter.

**4)** Take away the starter and bring the main course.

**5)** Return to check everything is OK and offer more drinks.

**6)** Return to take their orders for dessert (ask: "With cream, ice-cream or custard?")

**7)** Bring the dessert.

**8)** Prepare the bill while the customer is eating dessert.

**9)** Wait for the customer to request the bill, take payment and show the customer out (if they give you a tip).

**During the role play, the customers will have special characters. You should try to guess what is unusual about each customer.**

### Target language

**Waiter**

*Good evening Madam / Sir.*
*A table for 3 / 4 / 5 ?*
*What would you like to order?*
*Would you like...*
*to try the wine?*
*to order dessert?*
*Anything else?*
*Here you are.*
*Here's...*
*the menu / your starter / the bill.*
*Enjoy your meal.*
*Is everything OK?*

## Traditional restaurant – Customer A

**You are a customer at Bragg's English Restaurant.**

**Your character:**
You love this restaurant. It's your favourite. It was your idea to come here, and you're going to enjoy yourself, whatever happens. Order lots of everything!

**During the meal, try to guess what is unusual about the other customers' characters.**

## Traditional restaurant – Customer B

**You are a customer at Bragg's English Restaurant.**

**Your character:**
You love complaining about anything – food, music, chairs, other people, the weather, etc. Make sure you complain about everything in the restaurant!

**During the meal, try to guess what is unusual about the other customers' characters.**

## Traditional restaurant – Customer C

**You are a customer at Bragg's English Restaurant.**

**Your character:**
You love to talk, especially about food. Try to start a conversation about the food on the menu, and keep it going. Ask everybody's opinion, and agree with them as much as possible!

**During the meal, try to guess what is unusual about the other customers' characters.**

## Traditional restaurant – Customer D

**You are a customer at Bragg's English Restaurant.**

**Your character:**
You are very worried about your health, and what you eat. You have read lots of terrible stories about how all the food on the menu can be bad for the health. Don't forget to tell everyone!

**During the meal, try to guess what is unusual about the other customers' characters.**

## Traditional restaurant – Customer E

**You are a customer at Bragg's English Restaurant.**

**Your character:**
You are very mean, and hate spending money. Suggest a cheaper restaurant. Try to avoid ordering wine – get water. Order the cheapest things on the menu and try to get a reduction!

**During the meal, try to guess what is unusual about the other customers' characters.**

## Traditional restaurant – Customer F

**You are a customer at Bragg's English Restaurant.**

**Your character:**
You have never been to a restaurant before. Everything is new to you. Ask for explanations about everything, such as the menu, the different food, the knife and fork, etc.

**During the meal, try to guess what is unusual about the other customers' characters.**

# 2f Fast Food restaurant – Teacher's notes

## Time / Level
25–35 minutes / Elementary to Pre-intermediate

## Target language
**Grammar**
Contracted question forms (*Eat in or take away?*)
**Functions**
Placing an order (*Can I have...?*)
Complaining (*This cheeseburger is too cold!*)
**Vocabulary**
Food (*fries, doughnut, milkshake, ketchup*)

## Preparation
Copy the menu below (one per pair) and the role play cards A and B (one set per pair). Cut up as indicated. If you would like to do the whole class role play, increase the size of the menu below to A3 and make several copies.

## Lead-in suggestion
Put the following questions on the board for discussion in pairs followed by feedback:

*1) How often do you eat in fast food restaurants?*
*2) What do you usually order?*
*3) Do you like fast food? Why? Why not?*
*4) If you don't eat fast food, where do you eat when you are out?*

## Role Play instructions
**Option 1 – Pairs:** Give out one copy of the menu to each pair. Check any difficult vocabulary. Hand out the role play cards. Give the students 2–3 minutes to read the cards. Four possible situations are given on the customer's card. Tell them to start with the first one (the simplest). Start the role play when they are ready. When they have finished, they should swap roles and start again.

**Option 2 – Whole class:** To make the role play more authentic, turn the class into a fast food restaurant. Create a counter in the middle of the room and divide the students into customers and assistants. If you have a few more customers, it will make the restaurant busier. Give them the appropriate role play cards and 3 minutes to prepare. Put the A3 size menus on the wall behind the counter. Tell the customers to choose any of the situations, or to invent their own. When everyone is ready, open the restaurant!

## Follow-up suggestion
Students discuss how healthy fast food is:

*1) Do you think fast food is healthy? Why (not)?*
*2) How could the restaurants make their food more healthy?*
*3) Do you think children should be allowed to eat fast food? Why (not)?*

### Burgers

| | |
|---|---|
| **Hamburger** | 70p |
| **Cheeseburger** | 85p |
| **Chickenburger** | £2.25 |
| **Quarterpounder** | £1.80 |
| **Masterburger** | £2.75 |
| **Fish burger** | £2.95 |
| **Vegeburger** | £3.20 |

### Chicken sticks

| | |
|---|---|
| 8 | £2.45 |
| 6 | £2.25 |
| 4 | £1.85 |

### Onion rings

| | |
|---|---|
| regular | £1.20 |
| large | £1.50 |

### Fries

| | |
|---|---|
| regular | £0.85 |
| large | £1.00 |
| bonus | £1.20 |

### Meals
*(include fries and drink)*

| | regular | large |
|---|---|---|
| **Hamburger / Cheeseburger** | £2.95 | £3.25 |
| **Quarterpounder** | £3.50 | £3.95 |
| **Chickenburger / Masterburger** | £3.95 | £4.35 |
| **Fish burger** | £4.10 | £4.50 |

### Special Offer

**Bonus meal:** add on 30p

### Drinks

| | regular | large |
|---|---|---|
| **Cola / Orangeade / Lemonade** | £0.90 | £1.15 |
| **Orange juice** | £1.50 | £1.80 |
| **Mineral water** | £0.80 | £1.00 |
| **Tea / Coffee** | £0.80 | £1.00 |
| **Cappuccino** | £1.30 | £1.60 |
| **Milkshake** *(chocolate / strawberry / vanilla)* | £1.10 | £1.50 |

### Desserts

| | | |
|---|---|---|
| **Apple pie** | £1.50 | |
| **Doughnut** *(chocolate / cinnamon)* | £0.70 | |
| | regular | large |
| **Ice-cream** *(chocolate / strawberry / vanilla)* | £0.85 | £1.05 |

*Burger Master wish you a pleasant meal.*
*If you have any comments about our food or service, please inform our manager.*

 

# Fast Food restaurant



## Student A – Customer

**Situation 1**
You are a customer in a fast food restaurant. Go up to the counter and order lunch from the menu. You've only got £5.

**Situation 2**
You don't like ice in your drinks, ketchup, or too much salt on your fries. Place an order for two people. Your friend is coming soon. She is a vegetarian. You've only got a £50 note.

**Situation 3**
You are interested in the Masterburger. Ask: *What's in it?* If it sounds good, order one. You'd also like a milkshake, but you don't know what chocolate, strawberry and vanilla are. Ask the assistant to explain them.

**Situation 4**
You have just started your meal, but your cheeseburger is cold and your cola is too warm. Take them back to the counter and complain. Ask for another cheeseburger and another drink.

**Target language**

*I / She was first.*
*Do you have any special offers?*
*Can I have…*
*a hamburger / a cheeseburger? / a chickenburger meal?*
*large fries / a milkshake / cola / coffee?*
*without…*
*ketchup / salt / ice.*
*Have you got…*
*ketchup / barbecue sauce?*
*How much is that?*
*I want to eat in / take away.*
*This is too cold / These are too salty.*

---

# Fast Food restaurant



## Student B – Assistant

**You are an assistant in a fast food restaurant. It's very busy today. After you take the order, repeat it to the customer at the end, and tell him/her how much it costs.**

**Remember…**

- Don't forget to ask if the customer wants regular or large.
- Don't accept £50 notes. Ask for something smaller.
- If somebody has a special request (e.g. no ketchup) tell them they'll have to wait for 5 minutes.
- If anyone complains, say 'Sorry' and explain that it's very busy today. Don't give them their money back.
- Note: The Masterburger is a large cheeseburger with onion rings.

**Target language**

*Can I help you?*
*Who's next?*
*Would you like…*
*regular or large?*
*fries / a drink (with that)?*
*Eat in or take away?*
*Do you mind waiting 5 minutes?*
*Here you are.*
*Is that everything? Anything else?*
*That's £3.15.*
*Sorry. Have you got anything smaller?*
*Enjoy your meal!*

 

# 2g Out of stock – Teacher's notes

## Time / Level

40–50 minutes / Upper intermediate to Advanced

## Target language

**Grammar**

Demonstratives vs. pronouns (*These are out of stock.* / *No they're not.*)

**Functions**

Reasoning with someone (*Can't I... anyway?*)
Making suggestions (*Why don't I just...?*)
Apologising (*I'm afraid... I can't let you do that.*)

**Vocabulary**

Purchasing products (*model, refund, exchange*)
Adjectives to describe emotion (*calm, annoyed*)

## Preparation

Copy the main role play sheet and the role play cards for Customer and Assistant / Manager (one of each per pair). Cut up as indicated.

## Lead-in suggestion

Pre-teach the following vocabulary if necessary:

*out of stock; aerial; refund; printer cartridge*

Write the following question on the board for students to discuss in groups for 5 minutes:

*What do you think are the top 5 complaints about customer service in shops in the UK?*

Build up a list of the students' ideas, then give them the answers. You could even score points for the answers (e.g. 31 points for answer 1).

> **Answers**
> **1)** slow service / long queues (31%) **2)** problems with returning goods (17%) **3)** rude / inflexible staff (15%) **4)** staff with inadequate knowledge (9%) **5)** items out of stock (7%)

Find out if the students have recently had any of the above problems.

## Role Play instructions

A) Hand out the main worksheet, one per pair, and give them 3 minutes to read the conversation and answer the question in A. Check that they all understand the problem: The aerial was out of stock only on the computer system.

B) Tell the students to put one of the adjectives in each of the brackets to express the emotion they would be feeling.

C) Students practise performing the dialogue to express these emotions.

D) Put each pair of students with another pair. If necessary, create a group of six. Each pair should perform their version of the dialogue, and the others should try to guess the emotion after each line. At the end, get one or two pairs to come out to the front to perform to the whole class.

**Optional:** Draw the students' attention to the kind of expressions in the original dialogue that were used for the following functions (examples in brackets):

Making suggestions (*Why don't I just...?*);
Reasoning with someone (*Well, can't I buy it anyway?*);
Apologising (*I'm afraid...*)

Now hand out a set of the Customer and Assistant / Manager role play cards to each pair. Give the students 2–3 minutes to read their cards. Start the role play when they are ready. Encourage them to use the *Target language* expressions. When they have finished, they should swap cards and do the second role play. Get feedback on who had the most success as customers and who would make the most annoying assistant / manager.

**Acknowledgement**
Thanks to Shaun Sweeney for bringing the original article to my attention.

✂ - - - - - - - - - - - - - - - - - - - - - - - - - - - - - - - -

# Out of stock



## Customer

**Role Play 1**

One of your Soundblaster computer speakers has broken. You go into Dickson's, and you're in luck! There is one computer speaker left on the shelf. It's the same model and colour as yours. The price is £19.95 for 2. Take it to the checkout and buy it.

*When you've finished, swap role play cards with your partner*

**Role Play 2**

You bought a cartridge for your computer printer from Dickson's yesterday for £8.35. Unfortunately, when you got home and opened it, you found it was the wrong size. Take it back to the store and try to get a refund. The cartridge you need costs £8.60.

> **Target language**
> **Making suggestions**
> *Why don't you...?*
> *What about if I...?*
>
> **Reasoning**
> *Couldn't you just...?*
> *Look, I just want to...*
> *Can't I ... anyway?*
>
> **Getting angry**
> *I don't believe this!*
> *Are you being serious?*
> *Could I speak to the manager, please?*

 

# Out of stock

**A Read the conversation below. How would you react if you were the customer?**

A customer went into an electrical store to buy an indoor television aerial. She found one and took it to the checkout. The assistant tapped a number into the computer and the following conversation took place:

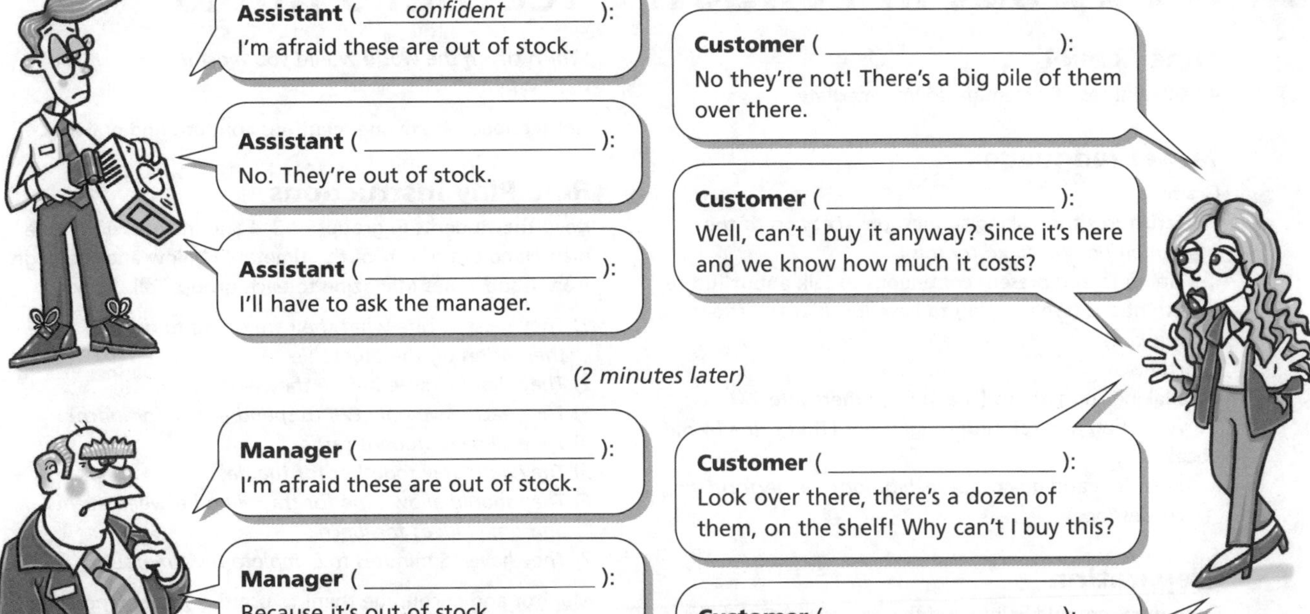

**Assistant** ( *confident* ): I'm afraid these are out of stock.
**Customer** ( ________________ ): No they're not! There's a big pile of them over there.
**Assistant** ( ________________ ): No. They're out of stock.
**Customer** ( ________________ ): Well, can't I buy it anyway? Since it's here and we know how much it costs?
**Assistant** ( ________________ ): I'll have to ask the manager.
*(2 minutes later)*
**Manager** ( ________________ ): I'm afraid these are out of stock.
**Customer** ( ________________ ): Look over there, there's a dozen of them, on the shelf! Why can't I buy this?
**Manager** ( ________________ ): Because it's out of stock.
**Customer** ( ________________ ): Look, I've got the exact money here. Why don't I just put it on the counter, walk away with the aerial and you can sort it out later?
**Manager** ( ________________ ): I can't let you do that. You see, it's out of stock.


A true story, adapted from *The Guardian* Saturday 11 June 2005

**B Now think carefully about the conversation and the emotions of the people involved. Working in pairs, choose one of these adjectives from the box below and write it in each gap. There are no right or wrong answers – you decide! You can repeat some of the adjectives if you like.**

| confident | surprised | insistent | calm |
|---|---|---|---|
| annoyed | firm | confused | thoughtful |
| sarcastic | stubborn | | |

**C Practise reading the conversation in pairs. One of you should play the role of customer and the other should play the roles of assistant and manager. Try to express the emotions you wrote.**

**D Act out your conversation for another pair of students. Don't show the other students the adjectives you wrote. After each line, they should try to guess the adjective. So act it out as well as you can!**

---

Role Plays for Today

# Out of stock

## Assistant / Manager

**Role Play 1**

There is only one Soundblaster computer speaker left. However, you can only sell them in pairs. The price for two is £19.95. **Also...** The credit card machine is broken. Don't sell anything without a receipt. You don't have any paper for the receipt machine.

*Now swap role play cards with your partner*

**Role Play 2**

A customer will bring a computer printer cartridge back today, but the package has been opened. No refunds can be given if the cartridge has been opened. Offer to exchange the product for something else. **However...** your manager is away today, and you don't know how to enter exchanges into the till. Tell the customer to try to find something at exactly the same price: £8.35. (In fact, the only item for this price is a mobile phone battery.)

### Target language

**Apologising politely**

*I'm sorry madam / sir.*
*I'm afraid...*
*...we can't do that because...*
*...we can only do that if...*
*...I can't let you do that.*

**Expressing uncertainty**

*I don't know.*
*I'm not sure.*
*The manager might know.*
*I'll just go and get him.*

 

# 3a A day out in London – Teacher's notes

## Time / Level
40–60 minutes / Elementary to Intermediate

## Target language
**Grammar**

Structures for making suggestions (*Let's go to the exhibition. We could try this.*)

*Going to* and present continuous to talk about future intentions (*We're going to have lunch at the street market.*)

**Functions**

Making suggestions (*Shall we go there later?*)

Accepting and refusing suggestions (*That's fine by me.*)

**Vocabulary**

Free time and going out (*exhibition, live performance, concessions*)

## Preparation
Copy the timetable below and the page from *Good Times* Magazine (one per group of 3–4 students). Cut up as indicated.

## Lead-in suggestion
Pre-teach any of the following if necessary: *concessions; that sounds (great); entrance fee; live performance.*

Put the students into groups of 3–4 and write the following question on the board for discussion:

*Which city in the world would you most like to visit for a day? Why?*

Get feedback. If anyone mentions London, find out why.

## Role Play instructions
Keep the students in groups of 3–4 and introduce the role play. Hand out a copy of the timetable below and the page from *Good Times* Magazine to each group. Tell them:

*1) They must decide what they are going to do, and write their notes on the timetable*
*2) They should agree before they write*
*3) They each have only £20 to spend (+ £10 for lunch)*
*4) They all have student cards*
*5) They must stay together for the day*
*6) They should allow time for travelling between events and time / ideas for lunch*
*7) They have 15 minutes to complete the timetable*

Monitor and encourage them to use the *Target language*. Help with vocabulary if necessary. Make sure they all contribute to the decision-making process.

## Follow-up suggestion
Students from different groups get together to tell each other about what they are going to do. They will need to see their timetables to help them remember. You can swap the timetables round every 2–3 minutes. Encourage them to use *going to* and present continuous, as these are arranged future plans / intentions.

✂ - - - - - - - - - - - - - - - - - - - - - - - - - - - - - - - - - - - - - - - -

# A day out in London

Role Plays for Today

**You have just arrived in London for one day only. It's summer and the weather's sunny! Choose activities from the magazine. Write your plans for the day here. You each have a one-day travelcard, £20 for activities and £10 for lunch.**

| Time | Activity | Cost (each) |
|---|---|---|
| 9:00am | | £ |
| 10:00am | | £ |
| 11:00am | | £ |
| 12:00pm | | £ |
| 1:00pm | | £ |
| 2:00pm | | £ |
| 3:00pm | | £ |
| 4:00pm | | £ |
| 5:00pm | | £ |
| 6:00pm | | £ |
| | Total cost per person | £ |

**Target language**

**Making suggestions**

*We could...* / *Let's...* / *Shall we...* / *Why can't we...* — *visit the...* / *go to the...* / *have lunch...?* / *try the...?*

**Agreeing and Disagreeing**

*This sounds good.*
*That's a great idea!*
*OK. That's fine by me.*
*I'm not sure that's a good idea.*
*Sorry, but I don't like...*
*That sounds really boring!*

 

***Exhibition of Italian Renaissance Art***
***Including works by Raphael & Michelangelo***

## National Gallery

**Trafalgar Square (Charing Cross Tube)**

Open Daily 9am to 6pm
Entrance fee: £3.50 (£2 students) Children: Free
Free Entry after 4:30pm

## Haymarket Cinema

Haymarket (Piccadilly Circus Tube)
Films Showing:

**Star Wars Episode 12 – The End of the Universe** (USA; 105 mins.)
**Dragonmaster** (Kung Fu action movie starring Bruce Chan: China/USA; 87 mins.)
**Il Postino** (The Postman: Italy, subtitled; 96 mins.)

*Start times – 11:30am, 2:15pm, 5:00pm, 7:45pm*
*Tickets: £8.00 (£5.00 students) 11:30am only.*
*£11.00 (£8.50 students) all other times.*

## Camden Lock Street Market

**(Camden Town Tube) Open every Saturday from 11:00am to 7:00pm Lively street market selling everything from clothes (new and second-hand), books, bric-a-brac, music, souvenirs and natural health medicine. 3 cafés selling food from all round the world.**

**Entrance to the market: £3.00 per person.**

**This Saturday at 1:00pm:**
***Live Performance of traditional African music from Mali***

Lunchtime Classical Music Recital
**This Saturday at 12:00pm**
**Organ Recital of Bach, Pachelbel and Handel**
Organist: Graham Weltricht

At St. Martin's in the City,
Trafalgar Square (Charing Cross Tube)

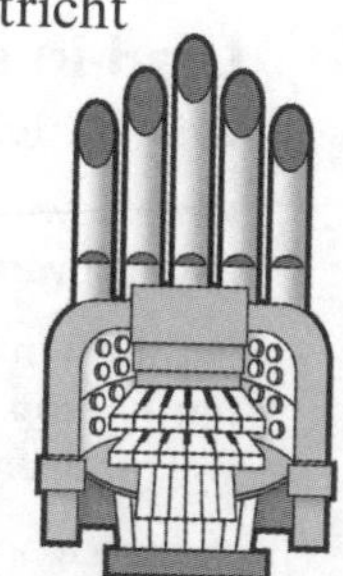

*Prices: £3.00; £2.00 concessions.*
*No children under 5.*
*Selection of sandwiches, cakes and drinks available from the church café (lunch not included in entrance price).*

## Medieval Games

Come and see the knights of the 7th century. Jousting, archery, sword fighting and a mock battle scene. Have your photo taken with the knights. Cost: £7.90; £4.00 under 12s (includes free medieval food and drink!)

**Saturday 3:00–5:00pm**
**at Regent's Park (Baker St. Tube)**

## Concert in the Park

**Hip Hop, Techno, R&B and Jungle performers from the US and the UK perform in Hyde Park (Hyde Park Tube) this Saturday from 2 until 5pm. Food and drink available.**
**Tickets: £8.00; £5.70 concessions. Over 18s only.**

**Tube map**
Travelling times – allow about 5 minutes per station.

Camden Town
Mornington Crescent
King's Cross St. Pancras
Great Portland Street
Baker Street
Euston
Farringdon
Barbican
Warren Street
Marylebone
Regent's Park
Euston Square
Russell Square
Goodge Street
Bond Street
Oxford Circus
Holborn
Moorgate
Marble Arch
Tottenham Court Road
Chancery Lane
St. Paul's
Covent Garden
Bank
Hyde Park Corner
Green Park
Leicester Square
Mansion House
Knightsbridge
Piccadilly Circus
Cannon Street
Sloane Square
St. James's Park
Charing Cross
Blackfriars
Temple
South Kensington
Victoria
Westminster
Embankment

## More ideas

**ANTIQUES FAIR**
(Oxford House, Oxford Circus Tube)
8:30am–4:00pm £4.00 entrance

**FOOD OF THE WORLD**
Food Tasting Event (Rose of York School, Baker St. Tube) 1:30–4:30pm
£8 entrance (includes 3 free dishes!)

**CHELSEA VS. ARSENAL**
5-a-Side Charity Football Match at Green Park (Green Park Tube) 3:00pm Tickets £7

**LONDON ZOO**
Open every day 10am–4:30pm Regent's Park (Baker St. Tube). £8.00 entrance

**KNIGHTSBRIDGE CAR SHOW**
continues until Sunday: Ferrari, Jaguar, Lamborghini, Aston Martin all on display – £8 (£6 concessions) 9am–5pm
Knightsbridge Tube station

# 3b Party strangers – Teacher's notes

## Time / Level

40–50 minutes / Pre-intermediate to Upper intermediate

## Target language

**Grammar**

Various

**Functions**

Using formal and informal spoken registers (*How do you do?*)

Introducing yourself (*Nice to meet you.*)

Showing interest (*Oh, really. Wow!*)

**Vocabulary**

Personal details and interests (*dance music, line of work, an MA*)

Informal English (*naff, stuff*)

## Preparation

Copy the *Create a personality* role play card (one per student) and conversations A and B (one set per four students). Cut up as indicated.

## Lead-in suggestion

Write the following task on the board:

*Write down 10 places where you can meet new people and have conversations with them.*

Put them in pairs and tell them it's a race. When one pair has 10, stop them and write a list on the board. *Weddings* will probably come up.

Pre-teach any of the following if necessary: *wedding; bride; groom; mingle; naff; folk.*

## Role Play instructions

Hand out conversation A to half the class, and conversation B to the other half, one copy per pair. If necessary, create a group of three. Instruct them to complete the gaps with the expressions in the box. Check the answers with the two halves of the class separately.

**Answers**

**Conversation A: 1)** How's it going? **2)** aren't they? **3)** That's true. **4)** What about you? **5)** Oh, really. **6)** Sure! **Conversation B: 1)** How do you do? **2)** Nice to meet you **3)** So, what do you do? **4)** Interesting. **5)** We've already met. **6)** Nice meeting you

Tell the students to practise reading their conversations in pairs. Then put two pairs together – one conversation A with one conversation B. If necessary, put three pairs together to make a group of six. Tell them to read out their conversations to each other and to decide which is more formal (B) and which is more successful (A), eliciting why. Now tell them to underline words or expressions used to show interest in both conversations, working in their groups of four. Write these on the board.

**Answers**

**Conversation A:** Right; That's true; Oh, really; Wow!; Sure. **Conversation B:** Right; Interesting. (Note: Sue is less interested in Terry)

Tell the students that they are going to go to a wedding reception party, where they can practise formal and informal introductions. Hand out a copy of the *Create a personality* sheet to each student and go through the instructions. It's best to get them to invent personalities, so that they really are 'strangers'. It also inspires creativity. Give them three minutes. When they are ready, ask them to stand up and let them begin. Tell them to try to remember everyone they meet. Background music will help to create a party atmosphere.

## Follow-up suggestion

In small groups, students discuss who they met at the party, what their jobs and interests were and who they got on with. Round up with group feedback.

---

# Party strangers – Create a personality

Role Plays for Today

**You are going to meet other people at a wedding reception. Create a personality for yourself. Don't use your real name or details:**

| Name: | Home City / Town: |
|---|---|
| Job: | Married? Family? |
| Favourite music: | Favourite drink: |
| How do you know the bride (Liz) or the groom (Gary)? | |
| What are your interests? | |

**Target language**

**Informal**

*Hi, there.* *All right.*
*How's it going?*

**Formal**

*How do you do?*
*Nice to meet you.*
*What do you do?*
*Nice meeting you.*

**Showing interest**

*Right.* *Sure.*
*That's true.* *Oh, really!*
*Interesting!* *Wow!*

**Stand up and meet the other people at the reception! Remember – if somebody starts a formal conversation with you, keep it formal. If you start a conversation, choose – formal or informal.**

 

# Party strangers

Role Plays for Today

**Put one word or expression from the box into each gap in the conversation:**

| That's true. | How's it going? | What about you? | aren't they? | Sure! | Oh, really. |
|---|---|---|---|---|---|

## Conversation A

**G:** Hi there. I'm Guy. 1 ______________________

**S:** All right Guy. I'm Sue.

**G:** Are you one of Liz's mates?

**S:** Yeah. We used to go to school together.

**G:** Right. So what do you think of the band?

**S:** They're a bit naff, 2 ______________________

**G:** Yeah. Good for the older folk, though.

**S:** 3 ______________________ Liz's parents are having a really good dance.

**G:** Yeah, her dad's quite a mover. So, what line of work are you in?

**S:** I work in a hairdressers on the high street. 4 ______________________

**G:** I'm studying for an MA, up in London.

**S:** 5 ______________________ What in?

**G:** Photography. I want to be a fashion photographer.

**S:** Wow! I love fashion! Have you ever been to any of the shows and stuff?

**G:** 6 ______________________ Actually, last night I was… (continues)

**Now read your conversation out to two other students, and listen to their conversation. Which conversation is more formal? How do you know? Which is more successful? Why?**

✂------------------------------------------------------------

# Party strangers

Role Plays for Today

**Put one word or expression from the box into each gap in the conversation:**

| Nice to meet you | Nice meeting you | Interesting. | We've already met. | So, what do you do? | How do you do? |
|---|---|---|---|---|---|

## Conversation B

**T:** How do you do? Allow me to introduce myself. My name's Terry Slater.

**S:** 1 ______________________ I'm Sue.

**T:** 2 ______________________, Sue. So, are you a friend of the bride?

**S:** Yes. I'm an old school friend.

**T:** Right. So what's your opinion on the entertainment?

**S:** Not my style, really.

**T:** I expect you like more modern music, do you?

**S:** Not exactly. I just don't like this band.

**T:** I see. 3 ______________________

**S:** I'm a hairdresser.

**T:** 4 ______________________ … I'm in advertising. I work up in London.

**S:** I hate London. It's too noisy and crowded.

**T:** Yes… It can be. Anyway, let me introduce you to my brother, Neil. He's just over there.

**S:** Don't bother. 5 ______________________ Look, I'll see you later, Tony. I'm just going to go and mingle.

**T:** Right. OK. The name's Terry, by the way. 6 ______________________ Susan. See you later.

**Now read your conversation out to two other students, and listen to their conversation. Which conversation is more formal? How do you know? Which is more successful? Why?**

 

# 3c Argument between friends – Teacher's notes

## Time / Level

20–40 minutes / Intermediate to Advanced

## Target language

**Grammar**

Question tags (*It was your idea to see this film, wasn't it?*)

Imperatives (*Don't lie! Shut up!*)

**Functions**

Making and refuting accusations (*It's your fault! That's not true!*)

Making up after an argument (*Let's just leave it there.*)

**Vocabulary**

Free time (*go out, nightclub, cinema*)

## Preparation

Copy role play cards A and B (one set per pair). For extra work on question tags, also copy the exercise below, one per pair. Cut up as indicated.

## Lead-in suggestion

Pre-teach: *(go) clubbing; on purpose; admit; avoid* if necessary. Put the following questions on the board for discussion in pairs followed by feedback:

1) *How often do you have arguments with your family or friends?*
2) *When did you last have an argument with someone? What about? Who was right?*

If you've recently done work on question tags, hand out the worksheet below to revise the forms and to show students how they could use them in this role play. When you've finished, remind the students that they should make up their own (different) dialogue for the role play.

**Answers**

*(in order)* wasn't it; did I; isn't it; shouldn't you; can I; didn't we; aren't I; are you

**Note:** When expressing emotion, intonation often becomes more exaggerated, nevertheless these tags are likely to have fall or rise fall intonation, due to the fact that the speaker knows (or thinks s/he knows) the answer.

## Role Play instructions

Students work in pairs, each getting one of the two role play cards. Give them time to read their cards before they begin. With intermediate classes, you could put the student As into pairs and the student Bs into separate pairs to prepare together, discussing the 'before the role play' questions. Make sure they make friends again at the end!

## Follow-up suggestion

Students in small groups brainstorm lists of Dos and Don'ts for having arguments:

| Do | Don't |
|---|---|
| Keep as calm as possible | Get violent<br>Contradict yourself |

---

Role Plays for Today

# Argument between friends
## Question tags in arguments

**1 Complete the gaps with the correct question tags:**

**A:** Hi!

**B:** Where have you been?

**A:** Am I late?

**B:** Of course you are. It was your idea to come to the cinema, __________?

**A:** Yes, but I didn't know that the film started at seven, __________?

**B:** That's why you're late, __________? You didn't want to see the film. And now I'm soaking wet!

**A:** Well, that's not my fault. You should have waited inside, __________?

**B:** I can't do that, __________? We agreed to meet outside, __________?

**A:** Did we? Oh, yes. Anyway, I'm here now, __________?

**B:** I don't believe this. You're not even going to apologise, __________?

**2 Listen to your teacher saying the question tags, and repeat. Listen carefully for the correct intonation.**

**3 Now act out the conversation in pairs.**

 

# Argument between friends

## Student A – Your role

You are student B's best friend. Tonight s/he wants to see a film, *Dangerous Instinct*. Unfortunately, you have already seen it, didn't like it and you don't want to see it again. The film starts at 7 o'clock and you arranged to meet at 6:45 outside the cinema.You arrive at 7:20 on purpose (but don't admit this to student B). You want to go to a nightclub tonight (Cosmos: only £4 entry before 8 o'clock) and you are already wearing your favourite 'clubbing' outfit.

**Before the role play, think about these points:**

- You need a good excuse to explain why you are late
- Why didn't you like the film?
- What will you do if student B still wants to see the film?
- How will you convince student B to come clubbing tonight?

**During the role play, make sure you ask student B...**

- Why did you invite me? You know I hated the film!
- Why don't we go clubbing instead?
- Could you lend me £4 to get into the night club? (You're broke.)

**Don't forget to make friends again at the end! (See *Target language*)**

### Target language

**Deciding fault**
*It's your fault (because...)*
*It's not my fault (because...)*

**Getting angry**
*That's rubbish! Don't lie!*
*Don't shout at me!*
*Don't interrupt me!*
*That's got nothing to do with you!*
*You always say that!*

**Question tags**
*I didn't know that, did I?*
*That's why you're late, isn't it?*

**Making friends again**
*I'm sorry I shouted at you.*
*Let me buy you a drink.*
*I'll try not to do that again.*

---

# Argument between friends

Role Plays for Today

## Student B – Your role

You are student A's best friend. Tonight you have arranged to see a film, *Dangerous Instinct*. You've never seen it before, but student A has (and didn't like it). You really want to see it, and you don't have any other friends to go with. The film starts at 7 o'clock and you arranged to meet at 6:45 outside the cinema. It's been raining and you're wet and cold. Student A arrives at 7:25! You are very angry. S/he probably arrived late on purpose to avoid the film. What's more, s/he is dressed up to go clubbing.

**Before the role play, think about these points:**

- Why did you want to see the film? Were you looking forward to the film?
- How are you feeling now? What are your feelings towards student A?
- Do you still want to pay to see the film even though it's already started?

**During the role play, make sure you ask student A...**

- Where have you been? Why are you so late?
- Why didn't you call me to say you'd be late?
- Why are you wearing your 'clubbing' outfit?
- How am I going to go clubbing in these wet clothes?
- Why don't you pay for the night club, since you were so late?

**Don't forget to make friends again at the end! (See *Target language*)**

### Target language

**Deciding fault**
*It's your fault (because...)*
*It's not my fault (because...)*

**Getting angry**
*That's rubbish! Don't lie!*
*Don't shout at me!*
*Don't interrupt me!*
*That's got nothing to do with you!*
*You always say that!*

**Question tags**
*I didn't know that, did I?*
*That's why you're late, isn't it?*

**Making friends again**
*I'm sorry I shouted at you.*
*Let me buy you a drink.*
*I'll try not to do that again.*

 

# 3d Telephone phone-around – Teacher's notes

## Time / Level

30–45 minutes / Pre-intermediate to Upper intermediate

## Target language

**Grammar**

Present continuous and *going to* for future arrangements / intentions (*We're meeting in the restaurant at 7.*)
*Will* for new decisions (*OK. So I'll call him.*)

**Functions**

Making and declining suggestions (*Why don't we…?; Actually, I don't really want to…*)

**Vocabulary**

Social events (*go out, night club, pub*)

## Preparation

Copy conversations 1, 2 and 3 (one of each per pair). Take a mobile phone into class if you have one.

## Lead-in suggestion

Tell the students to listen to one half of a phone conversation. Put these questions on the board:

*1) What is the conversation about?*
*2) How does the speaker use 'Is that' and 'This is'?*
*3) What arrangements does s/he make?*

Take out your mobile and pretend to call a friend to arrange a night out on the town. Start by using the above two phrases (*Hi. Is that Tim? Hi, Tim. This is Jason…* etc.) and ad lib the conversation. Elicit the answers to the three questions and write them on the board.

## Role Play instructions

Sit the students in a circle, and check that there is an even number. Participate yourself if necessary. Put the students into A–B pairs so that each A is talking to the student on their left (important!). Make sure they all know the names of the students on their left and right. Hand out a copy of conversation 1 to each pair. Tell them that they must perform the conversation, improvising the missing information appropriately (i.e. using their real names, deciding where they are going, etc.). Do a quick example, and let them act the conversation out in their pairs. Monitor to make sure they do it only once, and don't swap roles.

**Tip** If all the students have mobile phones, get them to pretend to use them. It makes the conversations and the body language much more realistic.

When they finish, they should understand that each B now needs to phone the person on their left (the A of the next pair). Thus they change partners. Give out conversation 2 and let them act it out in pairs. Note that in this conversation, they have to remember the details of conversation 1. Make sure that the Bs notice that they start the conversation.

Now the Bs have to call back their original A partner to try to reorganise the plans. Hand out Conversation 3. They will notice that they have to improvise the conversation from the third line onwards. Encourage them to use the *Target language* if necessary. They will then have to call back their other partner to try to reorganise their plans! This will go on for several more conversations. Monitor carefully, and, if necessary, speed up any pairs who are taking longer for their conversations than the others. Most groups will begin to agree on a set of plans after about 5–8 conversations, however this varies, and you will need to watch carefully to decide when to bring the activity to a conclusion.

## Follow-up suggestion

Put the students into pairs with someone who they haven't spoken to yet. Put the following questions on the board for discussion:

*1) Where are you going tonight?*
*2) Did you manage to agree with both your partners? Why (not)?*

It's fun to get feedback on the answers to these questions. Often there will be a lot of different ideas about who is going where with whom. If you like, get them to make spontaneous decisions **now** to finalise their plans once and for all.

 

# Telephone phone-around

Role Plays for Today

## Conversation 1

**A:** Hello. Is that (*name*)?

**B:** Yes, speaking.

**A:** This is (*name*). How are you?

**B:** I'm ( *?* ). And you?

**A:** I'm ( *?* ). Listen, tonight I'm going (*where?*) with some of the other students from our class. Do you fancy coming?

**B:** Er... What time are you going?

**A:** We're meeting at about (*time*).

**B:** Yeah, I'd love to come! I'll give (*the person on my left*) a call, to see if s/he's free. I'll call you back in 5 minutes.

**A:** Good idea. Bye.

**B:** Bye.

# Telephone phone-around

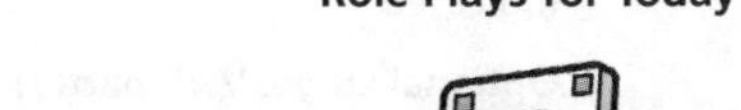

Role Plays for Today

## Conversation 2

**B:** Hello. Is that (*name*)?

**A:** Yes, speaking.

**B:** This is (*name*). How are you?

**A:** I'm ( *?* ). And you?

**B:** I'm ( *?* ). Listen, tonight I'm going (*where?*) with some of the other students from our class. Do you fancy coming?

**A:** Er... What time are you going?

**B:** We're meeting at about (*when?*).

**A:** I'd love to come, but I've already got plans. I'm going (*where?*) with (*who?*). We're meeting at about (*when?*). Why don't you come with us?

**B:** Er... That's a good idea. I'll just give (*who?*) a call to see if s/he's OK to change her/his plans. I'll call you back in 5 minutes.

**A:** OK. Bye.

**B:** Bye.

# Telephone phone-around

Role Plays for Today

## Conversation 3

**B:** Hello. Is that (*name*)?

**A:** Yes, speaking.

**B:** This is (*name*) again. Listen. I've just been speaking to (*who?*). Apparently, s/he...

*(Continue the conversation as necessary. You will need to make other phone calls to finalise your arrangements.)*

**Target language**

**Making suggestions**
*Do you fancy (verb+ing)...?*
*Why don't we (verb)...?*
*Actually, I don't really want to...*

**Talking about plans**
*We're meeting at...*
*I'd love to come!*

**Changing plans**
*Could you call her?*
*I'll call him and tell him.*

# 3e Flatmates – Teacher's notes

## Time / Level

50–60 minutes (+10 minutes for verb patterns)
Pre-intermediate to Upper intermediate

## Target language

**Grammar**

Verb patterns: verb + gerund; verb + infinitive; preposition + gerund (*I don't mind doing the washing. I want him to do the shopping...*)

**Functions**

Making suggestions (*How about if I do that?*)
Agreeing and disagreeing (*That's a good point.*)

**Vocabulary**

Housework and chores (*vacuum the flat, do the washing up, do the shopping*)

## Preparation

Copy the worksheet with the table (one per group of 3–4 students) and the four role play cards (one per student). Copy the *Memorising verb patterns* worksheet (one per group of 3) if you would like to do this as well. Cut up as indicated.

**Optional stage: Verb patterns**

If you would like to do some extra grammar work, put them into groups of three and hand out the worksheet below (Memorising verb patterns). Make sure they don't write the answers. They should try to process the information in real time! After they have done it once, get feedback.

**Answers**
*(in order)* cleaning; to cook; cook; cooking; doing; do; to do; ironing; doing; to wash; washing

Now get them to do it twice more, changing roles each time.

## Lead-in suggestion

Pre-teach the following if necessary: *housework; chores; do your fair share (of the work); ironing; repair; vacuum (v); rota.*

**Cultural note:**
If necessary, check that your students are familiar with the concept of flat sharing. If they've seen the TV show 'Friends', you could elicit the names of the characters, approx ages, background, etc.

Put students into groups of 3–4 (four if possible – see below) and hand out the worksheet. Tell them to discuss the five questions, followed by feedback (5 minutes).

## Role Play instructions

Read the introduction to the role play with them (on the worksheet). Tell them they are going to role play the meeting and point out the *Target language*. Give each student in each group a role play card. Leave out card D for groups of three, although groups of four are best if possible. When they are ready they can begin. The role play will take from 10–20 minutes, depending on level, group size and character.

## Follow-up suggestion

Reorganise the groups so that all the students who played role A are sitting together, and the same with role B, C, etc. Put the following questions on the board for discussion (imagining that they are still the person on their role play card) followed by feedback:

*1) Which jobs do you have to do in your flat?*
*2) Are you happy with this?*
*3) Did you argue about anything? Why?*

---



# Flatmates

## Memorising verb patterns

**Read out this conversation in groups of three. Don't write anything. Say the verbs in the boxes in one of three forms:**

**1)** verb + *ing* (e.g. *cleaning*) **2)** *to* + verb (e.g. *to clean*) **3)** verb (*clean*)

**Tara:** I don't mind **clean** the lounge, but I don't want **cook** dinner every day.

**Phil:** Why don't you **cook** dinner, Max? You enjoy **cook**, don't you?

**Max:** Yes. OK. But I can't stand **do** the shopping, and I haven't got a car.

**Phil:** Let me **do** the shopping. But I refuse **do** the ironing as well. Tara's much better at **iron**.

**Tara:** OK. I don't mind **do** the ironing. But who's going **wash** the dishes?

**Max:** Not me! I hate **wash** the dishes!

**Now change roles and read the conversation again. Try to do it more quickly this time. Then change roles and do it again, even more quickly! Correct any mistakes your partners make.**

 

# Flatmates



## Discussion

**1)** Who do you live with?

**2)** Who does most / all of the housework? Do you think this is fair?

**3)** Do you do your fair share? Could you do more?

**4)** Do you ever argue about doing the housework?

**5)** Are there any chores that you enjoy doing?

**Target language**

**Using verb patterns**
*I don't mind (verb+ing)*
*I'd prefer (not) to (verb)*
*I want him to (verb), because...*
*She's much better at (verb+ing)*

**Agreeing and disagreeing**
*Sorry. I don't agree with you.*
*That's a good point.*
*Let me do that. I don't mind.*

**Making suggestions**
*How about if I..., and you...?*
*Why don't you...?*
*Who wants to...?*

## Role Play

You have a problem. You have all been sharing a flat for a month, but it's very dirty because nobody ever does the housework or the chores. You are going to have a meeting to decide how to organise the work.

**The teacher will give you a role play card. Read it and remember the information. Then start the meeting. Your aim is to agree on who will do which chores and to fill in the rota below.**

| The chores | How often? | How long? | Who will do it? |
|---|---|---|---|
| Doing the shopping | *once a week* | *2 hours* | |
| Washing the dishes | | | |
| Cooking | | | |
| Cleaning the kitchen | | | |
| Cleaning the bathroom | | | |
| Cleaning the lounge | | | |
| Vacuuming | | | |
| Washing and Ironing | | | |
| Repair Jobs | | | |

## Flatmates – Student A

You want to organise a rota for all the chores, so that everybody does their fair share of the work. Student B has a car, which makes it easier for him/her to do the shopping. Student C is a builder, so s/he can do the repair jobs well. You hate cooking and cleaning, and you aren't very good at ironing. (If you have student D in your group, s/he is a professional chef.)

## Flatmates – Student B

You work very hard as a fashion designer and you are too busy to do much housework, but you don't mind paying someone else to do your share of the work. You are the only one with a car. You are a vegetarian, but student C often cooks food with meat, which you can't eat. You are good at ironing, but you don't want to wash everybody's clothes as well. Try to do as little housework as possible.

## Flatmates – Student C

You work as a builder, and you are very good at repairing things. You think everybody should do their fair share of work. You don't like student B because s/he is very lazy and never helps with the housework. You want him/her to do more of the chores or to move out of the flat. You like cooking, but only with meat. Vegetarians really annoy you. Try to do as little housework as possible.

## Flatmates – Student D

You work as a chef. But you don't want to come home and cook for your flatmates. Try to get out of the cooking, if you can. You can get food cheaply at a special discount shop, and you don't mind doing repair jobs. But you hate cleaning. You don't like student A because s/he is always telling everybody what to do. Try to do as little housework as possible.

 

# 3f Breaking bad news – Teacher's notes

## Time / Level

30–45 minutes / Pre-intermediate to Upper intermediate

## Target language

**Grammar**

Past simple (*He spilt champagne on your laptop.*)

**Functions**

Breaking bad news (*I'm afraid to say that I have some bad news about Fluffy.*)

Sympathising (*If there's anything I can do…*)

**Vocabulary**

Pets (*feed, cage, rabbit, budgie*)

## Preparation

Copy the worksheet *Bad News Day* (one per pair), role play cards A and B (one of each per pair), *More Bad News* below (one per pair), and the discussion questions below (one per 3 to 4 students). Cut up as indicated.

## Lead-in suggestion

Put the following questions on the board:

*1) When did you last get some bad news?*
*2) What about?*

Provide your own answer, using something quite light-hearted (e.g. you failed your cycling test). Tell students to discuss the questions in pairs. Monitor carefully, and be sensitive if any very bad news comes up. Get general feedback on the board, eliciting a range of topics for bad news (e.g. exam results, losing something, death, etc.). Hand out the *Bad News Day* worksheet (one per pair) and give them three minutes to read the e-mail and answer the questions in A without using dictionaries. Get feedback. If they aren't sure, focus their attention on the word 'land' (v).

**Answers**

A) Toby is a budgie. He has died, probably from the cold and / or old age.

B) Put them in pairs to work out the meanings of the expressions through context. Get feedback and clarify if necessary. C) Students discuss the questions in pairs, followed by feedback.

**Answers**

C) Maurice was probably on holiday. Marie was quite sensitive and she broke the news gently by telling the story first, and using 'pass away'.

**Cultural note**

In the UK people are often very attached to their pets. If this is different in your country discuss the following questions with the students:

*What animals do people often keep as pets?*
*Which animal makes the best pet in your opinion?*

## Role Play instructions

Introduce the role play and put the students into pairs: A and B. Give out the relevant role play cards and give them 2–3 minutes to read their cards. Monitor and help with difficult vocabulary. Before you start the role play remind them to use the *Target language* expressions, and to break the news slowly and gently. After they have both broken the bad news, but before they finish, give the *More Bad News* card to Mark. He should break this news to Nicky as well.

## Follow-up suggestion

Put a cline arrow on the board and as each pair finishes, get them to mark their partners' names on the arrow, and find out why:

Insensitive ←——|——→ Sensitive

Then hand out the discussion questions, one per group of 3–4 students. Give them 5–10 minutes to discuss, and get feedback at the end. Remember to be sensitive at this stage.

---

## Breaking bad news – Discussion questions

1) Have you ever had to break any bad news to anyone?
2) How did you break it – in a letter, over the phone or face to face?
3) Did you prepare what you wanted to say?
4) What is the best way to break bad news?
5) Some people break bad news for a living, such as crime support officers. Could you do this job? Why (not)?
6) When did you last give someone some good news?


## Breaking bad news – Discussion questions

1) Have you ever had to break any bad news to anyone?
2) How did you break it – in a letter, over the phone or face to face?
3) Did you prepare what you wanted to say?
4) What is the best way to break bad news?
5) Some people break bad news for a living, such as crime support officers. Could you do this job? Why (not)?
6) When did you last give someone some good news?


---

## More Bad News – Mark

While you have been talking to Nicky, the post has arrived. There was a letter with Nicky's exam results. Unfortunately, she failed all her exams. Tell her gently.


## More Bad News – Mark

While you have been talking to Nicky, the post has arrived. There was a letter with Nicky's exam results. Unfortunately, she failed all her exams. Tell her gently.

## More Bad News – Mark

While you have been talking to Nicky, the post has arrived. There was a letter with Nicky's exam results. Unfortunately, she failed all her exams. Tell her gently.


 

# Bad News Day



**A** **Read the e-mail.**

Who is Toby?
What has happened to him?

**B** **What do you think these expressions mean?**

*He perked up…*

*…he had passed away.*

*…for you to deal with…*

*…it was down to old age…*

**C** **Where do you think Maurice was when this happened?**

Do you think Marie was sensitive in her e-mail?

Did she break the news gently?

**D** **The teacher will give you a role play card. Read it carefully and work in pairs when you are ready. One of you will begin the role play by phoning the other one.**

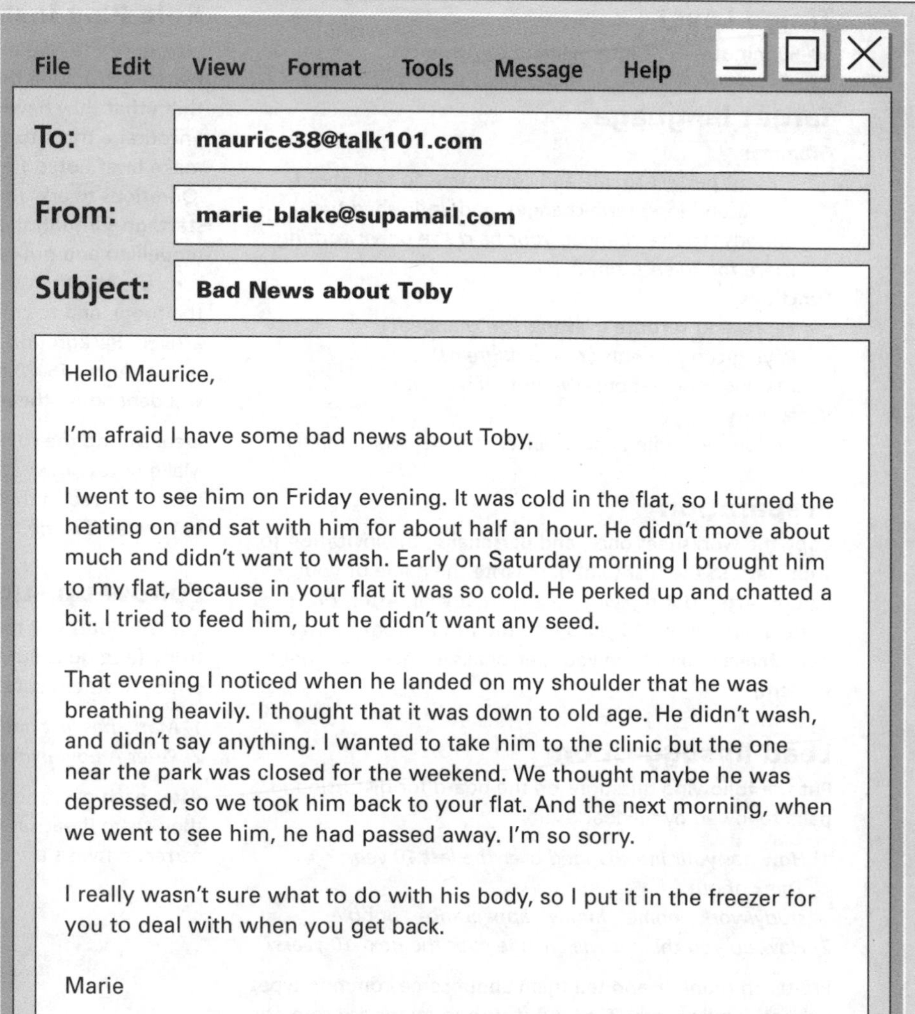


Hello Maurice,

I'm afraid I have some bad news about Toby.

I went to see him on Friday evening. It was cold in the flat, so I turned the heating on and sat with him for about half an hour. He didn't move about much and didn't want to wash. Early on Saturday morning I brought him to my flat, because in your flat it was so cold. He perked up and chatted a bit. I tried to feed him, but he didn't want any seed.

That evening I noticed when he landed on my shoulder that he was breathing heavily. I thought that it was down to old age. He didn't wash, and didn't say anything. I wanted to take him to the clinic but the one near the park was closed for the weekend. We thought maybe he was depressed, so we took him back to your flat. And the next morning, when we went to see him, he had passed away. I'm so sorry.

I really wasn't sure what to do with his body, so I put it in the freezer for you to deal with when you get back.

Marie

## Bad News Day – Student A (Mark)

Your friend Nicky asked you to look after her pet rabbit, Fluffy, for Christmas while she went away to her parents (she borrowed your new laptop computer when she went). Unfortunately, you lost the keys that Nicky gave you and you couldn't get into the flat to feed the rabbit for one day. So, you broke the window to get in, and fed the rabbit… but you gave it too much food. This morning, when you came back, it was dead.

You're good friends with Nicky, but she really loved her rabbit. Call her and break the news gently. You'll also have to explain why the window is broken. You could offer to buy her a new rabbit, if you think that's a good idea.

**Target language**

**Leading up to bad news**
*I have some bad news.*
*I'm afraid (that) I / he…*
*I'm sorry to say (that)…*

**After the news**
*If there's anything I can do…*
*I don't know what to say.*
*I'm so sorry.*

## Bad News Day – Student B (Nicky)

You are visiting your parents for a week at Christmas. You needed to do some work, so your friend Mark let you borrow his new laptop computer. Unfortunately, on Christmas Eve, when you were out, your dad spilt some champagne on it, and it stopped working. Your mum decided to try washing it… in the washing machine. It broke into little pieces. Mark isn't going to be very pleased. He was already quite angry that you asked him to look after your pet rabbit called Fluffy because he doesn't like animals.

The phone rings. Pick it up. Who could it be?

**Target language**

**Leading up to bad news**
*I have some bad news.*
*I'm afraid (that) I / he…*
*I'm sorry to say (that)…*

**After the news**
*If there's anything I can do…*
*I don't know what to say.*
*I'm so sorry.*

 

# 3g Meeting old friends – Teacher's notes

## Time / Level

50–60 minutes / Pre-intermediate to Advanced

## Target language

**Grammar**

Present perfect simple and continuous to talk about recent and long term changes, and unfinished time periods (*You've changed your hair! I've been working there for 3 years, now.*)

**Functions**

Expressing surprise (*Haven't you changed!*)
Paying compliments (*You look great!*)
Making observations (*I've put on weight.*)

**Vocabulary**

Various, including appearance, lifestyle, work, family

## Preparation

Copy the worksheet once, and personalise the invitation for your class. In the first (big) gap, write the name of your school. After 'during' write the current year. After 'on', write a date about 10 years into the future from today's date. Make copies from your personalised sheet (one per student).

## Lead-in suggestion

Put the following questions on the board for discussion in pairs followed by feedback:

*1) How has your life changed over the last 10 years?*
*Think about...*
*study/work home family appearance hobbies*
*2) How do you think it will change over the next 10 years?*

Pre-teach *reunion*, and tell them about some common types (school, family, work). Find out if such reunions are common and popular in their country and if any students have ever been to one.

## Role Play instructions

Introduce the role play and hand out the worksheets (one per student). Give them 3–5 minutes to read through. Tell them that they have 5 minutes to prepare their own future. Encourage them to think creatively, to be ambitious and to make brief notes. Refer them to the *Target language* 'Questions to ask' for more ideas if necessary. Before they start, go through the *Target language* expressions, modelling and drilling the correct intonation for showing surprise, etc. Then start the role play. Get them all to leave the room, and to come in one by one, as if they have just arrived. Background music will help get them into the mood! Allow 15–20 minutes for this stage. Exact timings will depend on the number of students.

**Idea:** During the role play, listen in on their conversations. Make notes on what everybody is doing and what changes have occurred in their life (*e.g. Maria has just had a baby boy, Peter is living in Los Angeles etc.*) See below.

## Follow-up suggestion

Use the notes you made during the role play to organise a true / false quiz. Put the students into teams of 3–4. Read out 5–10 statements, such as:

*1) Maria has just had a baby girl. (false)*
*2) Peter is now living in Los Angeles. (true)*

After each one, the students have 10 seconds to decide in their team if each is true or false. The team with the most correct answers are the winners.

 

# Meeting old friends



**A** Imagine that it is 10 years in the future. You see this advertisement for a reunion for the language school where you are now studying:

## ENGLISH STUDENTS' REUNION

_______________

Were you a student at the school during ___________?

Would you like to meet up with old friends?

Then come along to the reunion on...

_______________

***Free to all past students and teachers.***

***Please bring old photos of your time at the school!***

**B** You decide to go along and see your old friends. Before you do, decide on the following:

- What job do you have now?
- Where do you work?
  In your country?
  Abroad?
  Somewhere else?
- Have you become rich / successful / famous?
- Have you got married / divorced?
- Family?

**Think of some interesting things that have happened to you since you were at the school.**

- Where have you travelled to?
- What other languages have you learnt?
- Has your English improved?

**C** When you meet the other students, comment on how different they are. Use some of the *Target language* below. Try to speak to everyone.

## Target language

**Expressing surprise**

*Is that you, ______?*
*Good to see you!*
*What a surprise!*
*Wow! Haven't you changed?*

**Paying compliments**

*You look fantastic / great!*
*What have you done with your hair?*
*I love that colour!*
*It really suits you!*

**Making observations**

*I've / You've...*
*lost / put on weight.*
*dyed / lost my / your hair.*
*grown a beard.*
*changed my / your image.*

**Small talk**

*So... How are things going?*
*How's life treating you?*
*Fine! / Well! / Fantastic! / Terribly!*

**Talking about yourself**

*I'm living...*
*I've started...*
*I work for...*
*I've been working there for...*
*I've just changed...*
*I've got married...*
*Here's a photo of...*

**Questions to ask**

*Have you kept in touch with the other students?*
*How long have you been...*
*married / divorced?*
*living in ...?*
*a doctor / pop star?*

*Are you living in the centre of town?*
*Have you passed any English exams?*
*Have you done much travelling?*
*Do you know what happened to ...?*
*Do you recognise anyone else here?*
*Oh! Who's that? I've forgotten her name!*

 

# 4a Phoning for a job interview – Teacher's notes

## Time / Level

50–60 minutes / Pre-intermediate to Upper intermediate

## Target language

**Grammar**

Question forms, both direct and indirect (*How much is the salary? Would you mind if...?*)

**Functions**

Making polite enquiries (*Could you tell me...?*)

Describing personality (*I'm very organised.*)

**Vocabulary**

Work (*salary, position, duties, applicant*)

Personality adjectives (*patient, polite*)

## Preparation

Copy the worksheet with the job advertisement (one per pair), and the role play cards A and B (one set per pair). Cut up as indicated.

## Lead-in suggestion

Pre-teach any of the following as necessary:

*position; salary; duties; applicant; apply for; keen on; workload; work under pressure.*

Hand out the Job advertisement worksheet, one per pair.

A) Students think of five questions to ask about the job. If they think of more, tell them to note them down as well – they'll come in useful later.

**Possible questions:**

*What is the salary for the position?*
*What duties / responsibilities does it involve?*
*What are the exact hours?*
*How much training is given?*
*Are any qualifications necessary?*
*Whereabouts is the office?*
*Why has the position become vacant?*
etc.

B) Instruct the pairs to swap worksheets and check each others' questions. Monitor and check that the corrections are valid.

C) In pairs, students try to agree on the most important factors when phoning for a job interview.

D) The pairs compare with each other. If you have an odd number of pairs, split three pairs to make two groups of three. Encourage them to explain their choices.

## Role Play instructions

Tell the students that they are now going to role play a telephone call to arrange a job interview. Hand out role play cards A and B and give the students 2–3 minutes to read them. The human resources managers will need a little more time, so while they are reading, you can check with the applicants: *What is the aim of the phone call?* (To get a job interview – not the job itself) *What do you have to write down?* (The time, date and address for the interview) Start the role play when they are all ready. Encourage them to use the *Target language* expressions. Monitor and provide help with vocabulary if necessary. When they have finished, they should swap roles and start again. They can change partners if another pair finish at the same time, to enable them to respond to a different set of questions.

## Follow-up suggestion

Put the following prompts on the board:

*experience voice personality honesty ability*

Tell each student to provide feedback on how well their partner came across as an applicant, referring to these 5 points as they do.

**Note:** Another role play in this book, *Job interview 1* or *2*, would be a natural follow on from this one.

---

# Phoning for a job interview

Role Plays for Today

## Student A – Job applicant

You are very interested in the Office Administrator job. Phone up to find out more about it. Ask all the questions you prepared and any more that are necessary. Try to arrange a job interview if it sounds fine. Note down the time and date, and get the address of the office:

| Time of interview | Date |
|---|---|
| | |
| **Address of office** | |
| | |

**Target language**

*My name is...*
*I'm calling about...*
*Do you mind if I ask a few questions?*
*Would you like to ask me any questions?*
*Is it possible to arrange an interview?*
*I'm free any time next week.*

 

# Phoning for a job interview



**A** Have a look at this Internet job advertisement. It contains basic details about the job. If you were interested in the job, what else would you want to know? Write five questions in the spaces provided.

## Office Administrator
### for the Daily Word Newspaper

- ☑ *35 hours per week*
- ☑ *interesting work*
- ☑ *training given*
- ☑ *lively atmosphere*
- ☑ *salary on application*

Please e-mail: personnel@dailyword.co.uk
or call 020 0528 7810 for further information

*Closing date for applications: 3rd March*

1) ______________________________________________
______________________________________________?

2) ______________________________________________
______________________________________________?

3) ______________________________________________
______________________________________________?

4) ______________________________________________
______________________________________________?

5) ______________________________________________
______________________________________________?

**B** Now give your questions to another pair of students. They will check them for mistakes. It's important that your English is as good as possible when phoning for a job interview. First impressions count!

**C** Which of these factors is most important when phoning to enquire about a job? Put them in order (1–8):

- ☐ sound friendly
- ☐ be direct and honest
- ☐ be organised
- ☐ find out as much as possible about the place
- ☐ have a joke with them
- ☐ don't lie
- ☐ tell them all about yourself
- ☐ let them know you're really keen on the job

**D** Now compare with other students. Discuss your differences and justify your opinion.

✂ - - - - - - - - - - - - - - - - - - - - - - - - - - - - - - - - - - - - - - - -

# Phoning for a job interview

Role Plays for Today

## Student B – Human resources manager at the Daily Word newspaper

You need to hire somebody to replace the Office Administrator, who is leaving in three weeks.

### Position details

**Start date:** 15th March **Salary:** £23,000

**Hours:** 8am to 4pm Mon – Fri; 1 hour for lunch. Some evenings late.

**Location of office:** 28 Bridge Road (5 mins walk from the train station)

**Duties:**

- To send reporters to get news stories
- To contact politicians, celebrities, etc. and organise interviews
- To organise 3 meetings a day between editor and journalists
- To administer the office database, which controls all the staff, and their daily workload (training on database is provided)

**The correct applicant must...**

- have some computer experience, ideally with database administration
- be able to work under pressure every day
- be very organised, hard–working, polite and patient
- have an interest in news

***Note:*** *No specific qualifications are necessary, but all are useful.*

### Target language

**Giving information**

*The position begins...*
*The duties include... (verb)+ing...*
*You also need to... (verb)*

**Asking questions**

*What would you like to know?*
*Do you mind if I ask a few questions?*
*Do you have any experience of...?*
*Can you work under pressure?*
*Can you...?*
*How would you describe your personality?*
*Would you like to come in for an interview?*
*I'll give you the address.*
*I'll see you on...*

**If someone calls, answer their questions and find out if they have the necessary skills. Use the *Target language* to help you. If they seem suitable, arrange a date and time for an interview.**

# 4b Job interview 1 – Teacher's notes

## Time / Level

45–60 minutes / Elementary to Pre-intermediate

## Target language

**Grammar**

*Can* for ability (*I can use a computer.*)

Question forms (*Where do you work now?*)

**Functions**

Giving personal information (*Do you like working with people? Yes. I'm a very sociable person.*)

**Vocabulary**

Work (*salary, unemployed, CV*)

## Preparation

Copy the worksheet (one per pair, or one each).

## Lead-in suggestion

Write the following words on the board in random order:

*job you want this do why*

Ask the students to rearrange the words to make a question (*Why do you want this job?*). Elicit the most likely context for the question (*job interview*) and give them 4 minutes, working in pairs, to think up 3–5 more questions that could be asked at a job interview. Write these on the board. Find out how many of the students have been to a job interview recently, and how it went.

## Role Play instructions

A) Hand out the worksheet (one per pair) and tell the students to read the 12 questions and the five answers. Tell them to match each of the five answers to one of the questions. Avoid explaining vocabulary now; that comes in the next exercise.

| **Answers** A) 12 B) 6 C) 9 D) 1 E) 8 |
|---|

B) Now ask the students to look at the vocabulary in the box in B. Tell them to underline the same words in the questions / answers in exercise A. Give them 5 minutes to try to explain the words to their partner. Allow them to use dictionaries, and monitor. Elicit feedback and clarify if necessary.

C) Do an example for exercise C, by getting a student to ask you one of the unanswered questions, and providing an improvised generic answer. Then tell them to do the same with the remaining questions, speaking if possible.

D) In this activity, students are choosing a job that they would like to be interviewed for. Give them 3–4 minutes, and help with vocabulary. Check that each student has chosen one job, and then introduce the role play.

Read through the instructions in exercise E, and get two students to stand up and demonstrate the start of the interview. Start the role plays. Encourage them to use the *Target language* expressions. When they have finished, they should swap roles and start again.

## Follow-up suggestion

Students can tell the class if their partner got the job or not and why.

# Job interview 1

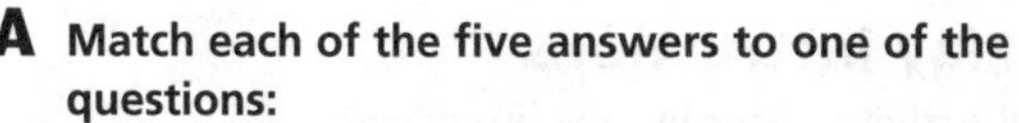

**A** **Match each of the five answers to one of the questions:**

**1)** What qualifications do you have?

**2)** Can you use a computer?

**3)** Can you drive a car?

**4)** What languages can you speak?

**5)** Where are you studying English?

**6)** Where do you work now?

**7)** Why do you want this job?

**8)** Do you like working with people? Why?

**9)** What salary are you looking for?

**10)** When can you start?

**11)** Do you have a CV?

**12)** Do you have any references?

**A)** Here is the name and address of my English teacher; and here's another one from my university. ☐

**B)** I am unemployed. I finished university two months ago, so I'm still looking for work. ☐

**C)** At least £20,000 per year. ☐

**D)** I have a degree in Economics from the University of Athens. ☐

**E)** Yes. They make a job more interesting. I'm a very sociable person! ☐

**B** **Check the meaning of these words. Explain them to your partner if you can:**

qualifications degree reference salary CV unemployed look for sociable

**C** **Now think of answers for the other questions. Practise asking and answering them with your partner.**

**D** **Which of these jobs would you most like to do? Why? Tell your partner.**

**SHOP ASSISTANT**
for a women's clothes shop
selling designer labels
40 hrs per week
*Central London*
❋❋❋

**TV NEWS REPORTER**
- travel the world for the BBC
- learn new languages
- 2-week trips
- *good salary!*

**RECEPTIONIST**
in a busy hotel
30 hrs per week
evenings only
some weekend work

**AMBULANCE DRIVER**
for a large hospital
day and night shifts available
45 hrs per week
**good salary!**

**E** **Interview your partner for the job s/he would like to do. Remember to ask the questions above. Think of other questions that are important for this job. Start your interview like this:**

**Interviewer:** Hello. Come in. I'm (name). Pleased to meet you.
*(shake hands)*

**Applicant:** Hello. I'm (name). Pleased to meet you.

**Interviewer:** Have a seat. Would you like a coffee?

**Target language**

**Applicant**
*Sorry, could you repeat the question, please?*
*That's a good question!*
*I think it depends on the situation.*

**Interviewer**
*Could you tell me about...?*
*Do you have any questions for me?*
*Could you give me an example?*
*What do you mean?*

 

# 4c Job interview 2 – Teacher's notes

## Time / Level

50–80 minutes / Intermediate to Advanced

## Target language

**Grammar**

*Can* for ability (*I can use a computer.*)
Present perfect for life experience (*I have worked as a receptionist before.*)
Question forms (*Are you good with people?*)

**Functions**

Giving personal information (*I'm currently working for a software company.*)
Describing personality (*Sometimes I can be a little too demanding.*)

**Vocabulary**

Work (*part-time, CV, wages, apply for*)
Personality adjectives (*reliable, friendly*)

## Preparation

Copy the worksheet (one per student) and *Starting the interview* below (one per pair – optional). Cut up as indicated.

## Lead-in suggestion

If necessary, pre-teach:

*strength; weakness; criticism; deal with; challenge; responsibility.*

Find out how many students have been to job interviews and what the jobs were. Then put the following on the board for students to do in pairs:

*Write a list of five tips for job interviews:*
*1) Wear smart clothes*

After five minutes get feedback and build up a list on the board, eliciting reasons for their choices. Other possible answers: *Be polite; research the company; ask questions,* etc.

## Role Play instructions

**Optional Activity – Starting the interview:**
Hand out the dialogue (one per pair) and give them a minute to read through. Do a demonstration yourself with one of the students. You take the part of interviewer. Make sure they stand up, shake hands and act it out well. Get them to swap over and do it a second time (without the dialogue if possible).

## Worksheet:

A) Tell the students that you have the five most difficult job interview questions. Elicit suggestions to see if they can guess what they are. Hand out the worksheet and tell them to match the questions to the answers.

**Answers 1)** C **2)** D **3)** B **4)** E **5)** A

Next, ask them to discuss the questions below for five minutes and get feedback.

B) Tell the students to find out from their partner what job s/he would like to do and to make notes in the box provided. Make sure they understand that this is **not** the job interview, just preparation. Refer them to the example, and encourage them to use correct question forms. Allow 8–12 minutes and monitor well.

C) Read through C with them, and get a few examples of possible questions using the prompts in the *Target language* box. Then tell them to decide who is going to interview who first. If possible, send the applicants out of the room, and get the interviewers to start by greeting the applicants in the corridor (as in the dialogue: *Starting the interview*), and then bringing them into the classroom for the interview. Allow 10 minutes for each interview, and swap them over after the first one.

## Follow-up suggestion

Students tell the class whether their partner got the job or not and why. You might also want to elicit which questions were most difficult to answer and why.

✂---

# Job interview 2
## Starting the interview

Role Plays for Today

**Stand up and practise the start of the interview with your partner. Decide what to say in the gaps (don't write). Shake hands when you meet. Smile and be friendly! Swap roles and do it twice.**

**Interviewer:** Hello! You must be ...

**Applicant:** Hello! Nice to meet you.

**Interviewer:** Pleased to meet you. My name is ... I'm the ... of the company. Come this way. Did you find the office OK?

**Applicant:** ...

**Interviewer:** Have a seat. Would you like a tea or a coffee?

**Applicant:** Yes please. I'll have a ..., thanks.

# Job interview 2



## A The five most difficult questions

**Match the answers A–E to the questions:**

1) What are your weaknesses? ☐
2) How do you deal with criticism? ☐
3) What do you think of your last manager? ☐
4) Why did you leave your last job? ☐
5) What salary are you looking for? ☐

A) What's the most you'll pay?

B) She had a very different personality to me, although I think we understood each other well. Sometimes she would offer good advice, and sometimes she would be a bit too negative.

C) I've been doing this job for a long time, so I don't really have any. Everything I do, I do well.

D) Actually, I'm used to it. So I deal with it really well. It's important to tell somebody if they're doing something wrong, and that's the manager's job, right?

E) It didn't challenge me enough. I wanted more responsibility, and nobody could offer it to me.

**Which are good answers and which are bad? Why?**

**Which is the best answer? Why?**

**Can you think of improvements for the bad answers?**

## B Preparation for the interview

**Ask your partner about a job that s/he would like to do. Don't start the interview yet! Make notes here:**

Example

**Job name:**
Fashion designer (Versace)
e.g. *What job would you like to do?*

**Location:** New York, LA, Paris (travelling)

**Hours:** 35–45 per week

**Duties:** design new clothes twice a year; train new designers; buy materials from all over the world; meet company director regularly; do interviews with the press

**Salary / wages:** £80,000

**Necessary skills:** ability to draw; ability to work fast, under pressure; creativity; ability to use a computer well

**Necessary experience:** 3 years in the fashion industry minimum!!

**Job name:** ____________________

**Location:** ____________________

**Hours:** ____________________

**Duties:** ____________________

____________________

____________________

**Salary / wages:** ____________________

**Necessary skills:** ____________________

____________________

____________________

**Necessary experience:** ____________________

____________________

____________________

## C The interview

**Now interview your partner for this job. Ask him/her lots of questions. Use the ideas from the Target language. Also, remember to ask the five most difficult questions!!**

**When you have finished, decide:**

1) Does she / he get the job?
2) Why? Why not?

**Target language – questions to ask:**

- *have / experience?*
- *what / duties / now?*
- *best skills?*
- *your personality?*
- *have / questions for me?*
- *job / now?*
- *hours / now?*
- *why / this job?*
- *your strengths?*

 

# 4d University interview – Teacher's notes

### Time / Level

40–60 minutes / Intermediate to Advanced

### Target language

**Grammar**

Future forms (*It will be interesting to study...; In 10 years' time, hopefully, I'll be working...*)
Question forms (*What are your strengths and weaknesses?*)

**Functions**

Expressing opinions and beliefs (*Obviously, it depends...*)
Responding politely (*I would say...*)

**Vocabulary**

Education (*applicant, research, degree*)
Courses of study (*structural engineering, business marketing*)

### Preparation

Copy role play cards A and B (one set per pair). Also copy the lead-in discussion questions below (one set per pair). Cut up as indicated.

### Lead-in suggestion

Hand out the lead-in discussion questions for students to discuss in pairs, followed by feedback.

### Role Play instructions

Put the students into pairs and introduce the role play. Ask each pair to decide who is going to be the first applicant. Hand out *Student B – Applicant* to all the applicants and give them one minute to choose a course from the list. Then ask student Bs to read the role play cards and spend a few minutes predicting possible questions and good answers. They should also look at the *Target language* on their role play cards.

While the applicants are thinking, hand out *Student A – Interviewer* to all the remaining students and tell them to prepare up to five questions specific to the course of study that their partners (applicants) have chosen. Give all the students 3–5 minutes for this preparation stage.

Start the role play when they are ready. You may want to ask the applicants to leave the room for a moment and arrange desks and chairs appropriately. The role play can begin with a formal (*How do you do?*) greeting.

When the first role play has finished, ask them to swap roles and repeat the preparation stage before enacting the second role play.

### Follow-up suggestion

In groups of 3–4 students discuss what was most difficult about the interview, and what their partner was like as an applicant or interviewer, followed by feedback to the teacher.

✂-----------------------------------------------------------------------

## University interview discussion

**Role Plays for Today**

**Discuss the following questions in pairs or groups of three.**

**1)** In your country is it easy or difficult to get into university / college?

**2)** What do you have to do before you are accepted? (qualifications? /application? /interview?)

**3)** Have you been to university?

**Yes**

**4)** What course did you study? Did you enjoy it?

**5)** Did you have to attend an interview?

**6)** If so, what do you remember about...

- how you felt before the interview?
- what the interviewer was like?
- what questions you were asked?
- how you felt after the interview?

**No**

**4)** Are you planning to go in the future?

**5)** What course would you like to study? Why?

**6)** Will you have to attend an interview?

**7)** What kind of things will your interviewer ask you about?

 

# University interview



## Student A – Interviewer for Rose University

**Before the interview, find out exactly what course the applicant has applied for. S/he may choose one of the following five courses:**

- English Language and Literature (including studying grammar and Shakespeare)
- Computer Science (including understanding how computers work and their future in society)
- Architecture (including structural engineering and building design)
- Business Management (including managing employees and starting your own business)
- Business Marketing (including understanding your customers, research and advertising)

**Think of 3–5 questions specific to this course. Write them below. During the interview ask 5–10 questions and note down the answers.**

### Target language: General questions (you can also think of others)

**1)** *Tell me about yourself.*

**2)** *How do you think a friend or tutor who knows you well would describe you?*

**3)** *Do you think that a university degree will get you a better job? Why (not)?*

**4)** *What do you see yourself doing ten years from now?*

**5)** *What problems will your level of English cause at the university?*

**6)** *What are your strengths and weaknesses?*

**7)** *Are you more comfortable following or leading? Why is that?*

### Subject-specific questions

1) ______________________________ ?

2) ______________________________ ?

3) ______________________________ ?

4) ______________________________ ?

5) ______________________________ ?

---

# University interview

Role Plays for Today

## Student B – Applicant

**You are about to attend an interview for Rose University. Choose one of the following five courses below:**

- English Language and Literature (including studying grammar and Shakespeare)
- Computer Science (including understanding how computers work and their future in society)
- Architecture (including structural engineering and building design)
- Business Management (including managing employees and starting your own business)
- Business Marketing (including understanding your customers, research and advertising)

**Before the interview begins, think carefully about the questions they may ask. They will ask questions, both on the subject you choose, and also general questions, such as:**

**1)** What do you see yourself doing ten years from now?

**2)** What are your strengths and weaknesses?

**3)** Are you more comfortable following or leading? Why is that?

### Target language

**Gaining extra time**

*That's an interesting question…*
*Let me think…*
*Obviously, it depends…*
*I would say (that)…*
*To be honest…*
*I'm not sure, but I think…*

**When you don't understand**

*What exactly do you mean by…?*
*Sorry, what was the question again?*

# 4e Enrolling at an English school – Teacher's notes

## Time / Level

45–60 minutes / Pre-intermediate to Upper intermediate

## Target language

**Grammar**

*Can* and *have to* to express permission and obligation (*You can enrol for 4 weeks. You have to take a test first.*)

*Would like* for expressing polite intentions (*I would like some information about...*)

**Functions**

Making requests and enquiries (*Could you tell me...?*)

Expressing rules and obligations (*All students have to take a test each month.*)

**Vocabulary**

Education (*intensive course, trial lesson, enrol*)

## Preparation

Copy the questions worksheet below (one per pair) and role play cards A and B (one set per pair). Cut up as indicated.

## Lead-in suggestion

Ask the students to discuss the following question in pairs:

*Why did you choose this school?*

Get feedback and build up a list on the board. Useful vocabulary will come up. If necessary, also teach:

*facilities; trial lesson; qualified; certificate.*

Hand out the questions worksheet below and instruct the students to complete exercise A. Check the answers when they've finished.

**Answers**

**1)** R **2)** S **3)** S **4)** R **5)** R **6)** S **7)** R **8)** R **9)** S **10)** S **11)** R **12)** S/R **13)** R **14)** S **15)** S

Then instruct the students to complete exercise B and get feedback afterwards, especially on the reasons for their choices.

## Role Play instructions

Introduce the role play, put the students into pairs: A and B, and hand out the relevant role play cards. The receptionists (Bs) will need some time to read through the information about the school. While they are doing this the As should write down five important questions to ask during the role play. Lower level students can copy from the questions worksheet, and higher level students can think of more questions. Monitor and help with any difficult vocabulary or questions. Point out the *Target language* to the students. Tell the Bs to 'think of a good answer' (i.e. improvise) if the students ask them about anything not on the role card. Also remind them to do the speaking test at the bottom of their role card with the student. After about 5 minutes they should be ready to start the role play. When they have finished they should swap roles and start again.

## Follow-up suggestion

Find out from the students what level they were given in the speaking test and whether they were happy with this. Also find out if they thought it was a good school and whether they would like to enrol or not. Elicit reasons for their answers.

✂-------------------------------------------------------------------

# Enrolling at an English school

**Role Plays for Today**

**A Look at these questions. Which ones are asked by the student? Which ones are asked by the school receptionist? Write S = student or R = receptionist. One question could be either.**

1) Have you studied English before? ☐
2) Are all the teachers qualified? ☐
3) Is it possible to pay by bank transfer? ☐
4) Why would you like to study English? ☐
5) What areas of your English would you like to improve? ☐
6) Are there any school rules? ☐
7) What do you find most difficult about learning English? ☐
8) How long would you like to study for? ☐
9) How do you test my level? ☐
10) Can I get a certificate when I finish? ☐
11) Have you had a look at our brochure? ☐
12) Do you have a price list? ☐
13) What time of day would you like to study? ☐
14) Can I have a trial lesson? ☐
15) What facilities do you have for students? ☐

**B Now look at the student questions. Underline the three most important ones. Tell your partner why they are important.**

 

# Enrolling at an English school



## Student A – Student

Your friend recommended the Dickens School of English to you. Find out about it, using some of the questions you have just studied. If it sounds OK, take the speaking test and organise for a trial lesson. Before you start, note down five very important questions that you would like to ask:

1) ______________________________ ?

2) ______________________________ ?

3) ______________________________ ?

4) ______________________________ ?

5) ______________________________ ?

**Target language**

*I would like some information about...*
*Could you explain about...?*
*Could you write that down?*
*Do you have...?*
*How much is...?*
*Sorry, could you repeat that please?*
*Thank you. I'll think about it.*
*I'd like to enrol.*

✂ - - - - - - - - - - - - - - - - - - - -

# Enrolling at an English school

Role Plays for Today

## Student B – Receptionist

You work for the Dickens School of English. Offer help and advice to any students who come into the school. Remember to answer their questions. If they would like to take a trial lesson, they must complete the test. Do the speaking test with them now. All the information you need is here:

## The Dickens School of English

| Number of weeks | General English (15 hours per week) | Intensive General English (30 hours per week) | Business English (15 hours per week) | Conversation Classes (10 hours per week) |
|---|---|---|---|---|
| 2 | £150 | £280 | £200 | £120 |
| 4 | £280 | £540 | £360 | £220 |
| 8 | £540 | £1020 | £680 | £400 |
| 20 | £980 | £1890 | £1350 | £760 |
| 36 | £1490 | £2790 | £1800 | £1040 |

**Times** Classes from 9–12 (mornings), 1–4 (afternoons), 5–8 (evenings) Mon–Fri

**Levels** 2) Elementary; 3) Pre-intermediate; 4) Intermediate; 5) Upper intermediate; 6) Advanced

**Payment Methods** Cash, credit card, or bank transfer (no cheques)

**Teacher qualifications** All teachers are fully-qualified with at least 1 year's experience.

**Rules** No smoking or alcohol in the school. No mobile phones in class. Speak only English in class.

**Student facilities** Library for study, listening and computer study; Internet café – free internet access, food and drinks; Student Bar – for social events (e.g. Pub Quiz Night, Karaoke Night – two events every month)

**How to change level** Students take a test each month. The teacher looks at the test results and decides who needs to change.

**Trial lessons** All students can have 1 free trial lesson after doing the test.

**Certificates** All students receive certificates at the end of their course.

### Speaking Test

**All students have to take a written test, but you can do the speaking test now. Ask the student these questions. Make notes and decide what level they are:**

**1)** Have you studied English before?
**2)** Why do you want to study English?
**3)** Why did you choose our school?
**4)** What areas of your English do you want to improve?
**5)** What do you find most difficult about learning English?
**6)** What is your hobby? Can you tell me about it, please?
**7)** What was the last book you read? Can you tell me all about it, please?

**LEVEL:** ______________________

**Target language**

*All students have to... (+ verb)*
*Students can... (+ verb)*
*Students can't... (+ verb)*
*If you want to..., you can...*
*Let's do the speaking test now.*
*Your level is Elementary / Pre-intermediate...*
*Thank you. Please come back soon!*

 

# 4f International business etiquette – Teacher's notes

## Time / Level
60–80 minutes / Intermediate to Advanced

## Target language
**Grammar**

Modal verbs to express obligation, prohibition and possibility (*We could reduce the price if...*)
Comparatives (*Our cars are much safer.*)

**Functions**

Introducing yourself formally (*How do you do?*)
Negotiating (*Could you increase your order? We can't go any lower than...*)

**Vocabulary**

Business (*representative, win the contract, drop your price, buyer, seller*)
Cars (*top speed, 6 speed, fuel, sun roof*)

## Preparation
Copy the worksheet (one per student).

Copy the four cards (*Brazil, China, Italy, Saudi Arabia*) – one per student. Don't worry if you don't have an exact multiple of four students, just make sure each student has one of the four cards (see below).

## Lead-in suggestion
Hand out the worksheet – *International business etiquette* – one per student. Read through the instructions for exercise 1, and then give them 3 minutes to complete it. They should then compare ideas in pairs. Get feedback.

Now create groups of 4–7 students.

Distribute cards A–D evenly in each group. If you have 5–7 students in a group, some of them will obviously get the same card and will be working in pairs as a team. This is no problem.

Tell them to read the *Business Etiquette* section on their cards only. Give them 3 minutes. When they have done this, instruct them to tell each other about business etiquette in the different countries, and to answer the three questions in exercise 2 on the worksheet. Get feedback.

## Role Play instructions
Introduce the role play. Tell the students that they are from the country they read about in exercise 2 (i.e. the students who read about Brazil are now from Brazil, etc.). Read through exercise 3 on the worksheet with them. Tell them to read the Role Play section on their cards and also to read about the two cars. Give them 5 minutes. Monitor and help with vocabulary, and check that they understand their aims for the meeting:

*The buyers need to get the lowest prices possible, ideally by getting the sellers to compete with each other. The sellers need to sell as many cars as possible to both buyers at the highest price possible.*

Point out the *Target language* on the worksheet to all the students.

**Idea:** Give out small slips of paper and tell the students to make business cards for themselves.

Tell the buyers (Italian and Saudi contingents) to leave the room and remind the sellers of the importance of impressing the buyers by showing an understanding of their culture. Remind them that it's a good idea to start with introductions and small talk before getting down to business (see *Target language*). Invite the buyers back in (if you have more than one group, make sure the sellers find the buyers from their group) and let the role play begin. Give the students plenty of freedom to conduct the meetings as they like. The role play could last anything from 15–30 minutes. Make a note yourself of any recurring mistakes to go over during the feedback session later.

## Follow-up suggestion
Ask the students who they thought was best at:

- negotiating
- playing their 'role'
- showing understanding of other cultures

If you made notes of recurring mistakes, you can provide feedback on these now.

 

# International business etiquette Worksheet



**1** **In your country which of these should and shouldn't be done in a business meeting? Write ✔ if it should be done, ✘ if it shouldn't be done and ? if it depends (make a note of what it depends on).**

- ☐ shake hands at the start of the meeting
- ☐ kiss or use first names if you know someone well
- ☐ present your business card first
- ☐ stand at least 2 metres apart
- ☐ make a few jokes to lighten the atmosphere
- ☐ don't look anyone in the eye for too long
- ☐ smile lots
- ☐ dress formally
- ☐ ask about someone's family to break the ice

**Compare answers with another student. If you are from the same country, discuss any differences of opinion. If you are from different countries, explain about your culture.**

**2** **The teacher will give you information about business etiquette in one of several countries. Read the information and then tell the other students in your group about it. Answer these questions:**

- Which countries seem to have similar business etiquette?
- Which seem to be quite different?
- What problems could this cause?

**3** You are going to take part in a business meeting role play. The meeting, in London, includes representatives from several countries trying to buy and sell cars. Read the information about your nationality, your company and what your aims are for the meeting. Study the two different cars on offer. When you are ready, let the teacher know, and you can begin the role play.

**Target language**

*How do you do? Pleased to meet you.*
*So, how was your journey?*
*Is this your first time in London?*

**Negotiating – Sellers**

*Our cars are safer / more reliable.*
*We could reduce the price by 5% if…*
*Sorry, we can't go any lower than…*

**Negotiating – Buyers**

*Is that your lowest price?*
*What else can you offer?*
*Would it be possible to…?*
*What about if we…?*

✂ - - - - - - - - - - - - - - - - - - - -

# International business etiquette Worksheet

Role Plays for Today

**1** **In your country which of these should and shouldn't be done in a business meeting? Write ✔ if it should be done, ✘ if it shouldn't be done and ? if it depends (make a note of what it depends on).**

- ☐ shake hands at the start of the meeting
- ☐ kiss or use first names if you know someone well
- ☐ present your business card first
- ☐ stand at least 2 metres apart
- ☐ make a few jokes to lighten the atmosphere
- ☐ don't look anyone in the eye for too long
- ☐ smile lots
- ☐ dress formally
- ☐ ask about someone's family to break the ice

**Compare answers with another student. If you are from the same country, discuss any differences of opinion. If you are from different countries, explain about your culture.**

**2** **The teacher will give you information about business etiquette in one of several countries. Read the information and then tell the other students in your group about it. Answer these questions:**

- Which countries seem to have similar business etiquette?
- Which seem to be quite different?
- What problems could this cause?

**3** You are going to take part in a business meeting role play. The meeting, in London, includes representatives from several countries trying to buy and sell cars. Read the information about your nationality, your company and what your aims are for the meeting. Study the two different cars on offer. When you are ready, let the teacher know, and you can begin the role play.

**Target language**

*How do you do? Pleased to meet you.*
*So, how was your journey?*
*Is this your first time in London?*

**Negotiating – Sellers**

*Our cars are safer / more reliable.*
*We could reduce the price by 5% if…*
*Sorry, we can't go any lower than…*

**Negotiating – Buyers**

*Is that your lowest price?*
*What else can you offer?*
*Would it be possible to…?*
*What about if we…?*

 

# Card A – **Brazil**

## Business Etiquette

Brazilians are warm, friendly and sociable. Brazil has many different races and ethnic groups. The families are close, as are business partners. They love to mix business with pleasure!

- The Brazilians love to stand close. Touching is a natural part of having fun
- Shake hands on meeting for the first time
- You can use first names at a business meeting
- Look Brazilians in the eye when you talk to them
- Invite them out for a drink after a meeting
- You can talk about any topic with Brazilians, as long as you are sincere about it

## Role Play

### Recife Cars from Brazil

You are the Brazilian representatives of Recife Cars. You are in London for a very important business meeting. You need to sell your cars to the buyers. Find out why they need cars, how many they need and tell them why your car is best. You will be competing with another car company from China (see *The 2 Cars*). If necessary, you can drop your price a little (by $700 per car), but try to win the contract at the best price possible. You can add extras or take away unnecessary features. Remember to impress the buyers by showing an understanding of their culture.

# The 2 Cars

**From Brazil (your car):**

## The Recife Samba!

**Features**
**Top speed:** 240km/h
**Fuel:** 8.4 litres per 100 km
**Safety:** 5/10*
**Reliability:** 7/10*
**Extras:** radio, sun roof, 6 speed

**Trade Prices**
**$17,400 each** (minimum 1000 cars)
**$18,100 each** (minimum 500 cars)

* according to *Car Buyer* magazine

**From China:**

## The CMI Shanghai

**Features**
**Top speed:** 225km/h
**Fuel:** 8.0 litres per 100 km
**Safety:** 6/10*
**Reliability:** 6/10*
**Extras:** CD player, car alarm

**Trade Prices**
**$16,800 each** (minimum 1000 cars)
**$17,800 each** (minimum 500 cars)

* according to *Car Buyer* magazine

# Card B – **China**

## Business Etiquette

China has a long and important history. The Chinese have been doing business for thousands of years. They can be very superstitious and may prefer to do things a particular way!

- Don't touch, except for the first handshake, or stand too close
- Introduce yourself and colleagues carefully. This is a sign of respect
- Keep your fingers away from your mouth
- Don't ask about politics in China
- Asking somebody about their hometown and its history is a good way to start a conversation
- Too much smiling is a sign of stupidity

## Role Play

### CMI Cars from China

You are the Chinese representatives of CMI Cars. You are in London for a very important business meeting. You need to sell your cars to the buyers. Find out why they need cars, how many they need and tell them why your car is best. You will be competing with another car company, from Brazil (see *The 2 Cars*). If necessary, you can drop your price a little (by $500 per car), but try to win the contract at the best price possible. You can add extras or take away unnecessary features. Remember to impress the buyers by showing an understanding of their culture.

# The 2 Cars

**From Brazil:**

## The Recife Samba!

**Features**
**Top speed:** 240km/h
**Fuel:** 8.4 litres per 100 km
**Safety:** 5/10*
**Reliability:** 7/10*
**Extras:** radio, sun roof, 6 speed

**Trade Prices**
**$17,400 each** (minimum 1000 cars)
**$18,100 each** (minimum 500 cars)

* according to *Car Buyer* magazine

**From China (your car):**

## The CMI Shanghai

**Features**
**Top speed:** 225km/h
**Fuel:** 8.0 litres per 100 km
**Safety:** 6/10*
**Reliability:** 6/10*
**Extras:** CD player, car alarm

**Trade Prices**
**$16,800 each** (minimum 1000 cars)
**$17,800 each** (minimum 500 cars)

* according to *Car Buyer* magazine

# Card C – **Italy**

## Business Etiquette

Italians are naturally sociable! Strong family ties and long friendships are typical! An Italian business partner is a partner for life.

- Meetings are never hurried
- Flexibility in negotiation is important
- Jokes are a good way to make friends
- Food and football are great topics of conversation
- Don't talk about the mafia or poverty in the south
- Use your hands when talking to Italians, it shows personality!
- Shake hands when meeting in business
- Don't stand too far away from a business partner, about 1 metre shows you are friendly

## Role Play

### Milan Car Rentals from Italy

You represent a car rental company from Italy. You need to buy 700 new cars for Milan Car Rentals, and you have been sent to a business meeting in London to choose from 2 different cars (see *The 2 Cars*). Look carefully at the information and discuss the good points and the bad points of the 2 cars. You want to spend about $17,000 per car, but you can increase this if necessary. Make sure you get the right cars and the best deal. Choose a business partner who understands your culture.

# The 2 Cars

**From Brazil:**

## The Recife Samba!

**Features**

**Top speed:** 240km/h
**Fuel:** 8.4 litres per 100 km
**Safety:** 5/10*
**Reliability:** 7/10*
**Extras:** radio, sun roof, 6 speed

**Trade Prices**

**$17,400 each** (minimum 1000 cars)
**$18,100 each** (minimum 500 cars)

*according to *Car Buyer* magazine

**From China:**

## The CMI Shanghai

**Features**

**Top speed:** 225km/h
**Fuel:** 8.0 litres per 100 km
**Safety:** 6/10*
**Reliability:** 6/10*
**Extras:** CD player, car alarm

**Trade Prices**

**$16,800 each** (minimum 1000 cars)
**$17,800 each** (minimum 500 cars)

*according to *Car Buyer* magazine

---

# Card D – **Saudi Arabia**

## Business Etiquette

Saudis are very hospitable, and like to be taken care of as guests. Many social formalities come from ancient Arabic customs.

- Don't stand with your hands in your pockets
- Never show the bottom of your feet when sitting down
- If you show too much interest in a watch or vase of a Saudi friend, they may feel obliged to give it to you
- Try not to turn your back on a host or important customer at any time – it's considered rude
- Don't make too many jokes at a business meeting
- Talk about cars, the weather or the family to break the ice

## Role Play

### Riyadh Taxis from Saudi Arabia

You represent a taxi company from Saudi Arabia. You need to buy 800 new cars for Riyadh Taxis, and you have been sent to a business meeting in London to choose from two different cars (see *The 2 Cars*). Look carefully at the information and discuss the good points and the bad points of the 2 cars. You want to spend about $16,000 per car, but you can increase this if necessary. Make sure you get the right cars and the best deal. Choose a business partner who understands your culture.

# The 2 Cars

**From Brazil:**

## The Recife Samba!

**Features**

**Top speed:** 240km/h
**Fuel:** 8.4 litres per 100 km
**Safety:** 5/10*
**Reliability:** 7/10*
**Extras:** radio, sun roof, 6 speed

**Trade Prices**

**$17,400 each** (minimum 1000 cars)
**$18,100 each** (minimum 500 cars)

*according to *Car Buyer* magazine

**From China:**

## The CMI Shanghai

**Features**

**Top speed:** 225km/h
**Fuel:** 8.0 litres per 100 km
**Safety:** 6/10*
**Reliability:** 6/10*
**Extras:** CD player, car alarm

**Trade Prices**

**$16,800 each** (minimum 1000 cars)
**$17,800 each** (minimum 500 cars)

*according to *Car Buyer* magazine

# 4g Finding accommodation – Teacher's notes

## Time / Level

45–60 minutes / Pre-intermediate to Upper intermediate

## Target language

**Grammar**

Modal verbs of obligation and prohibition (*You can't smoke, except in your room.*)

*There is / are* for describing rooms (*There's a bed, a wardrobe and a desk in the room.*)

**Functions**

Describing a room (*It's quite big, with two windows.*)

Expressing rules (*Pets are not allowed.*)

Making an appointment (*What about Monday at 6:30?*)

**Vocabulary**

Houses and furniture (*wardrobe, furnished*)

## Preparation

Copy the *Finding accommodation* worksheet (one per pair) and the role play sheet (one per student).

## Lead-in suggestion

Pre-teach:

*tenant; ad; landlord / landlady; flat / housemate; bills; deposit*

Ask the students what the best way to find rented accommodation in their country is. Elicit various means (newspaper, letting-agents, Internet) and find out if any students are currently living in rented accommodation. Introduce the role play and hand out the *Finding accommodation* worksheet. Ask them to do exercise A first to check the vocabulary.

**Answers**

**a)** Tube **b)** inclusive (of bills) **c)** exclusive **d)** pw
**e)** basement **f)** fully-furnished **g)** double glazed
**h)** mod cons **i)** spacious **j)** fully / newly-fitted (kitchen)
**k)** en suite (bathroom)

B) Tell students to discuss the advantages and disadvantages of each room, and to choose the two that they think are most promising. Tell them to write questions that they would like to ask at the bottom of the sheet. Get feedback after 5 minutes, writing the questions on the board as you do.

## Role Play instructions

Tell them that in 5 minutes they are each going to phone up about one of the two rooms they liked, and that they should decide who is going to be the landlord / landlady of each. Hand out a copy of the role play sheet to each student and give them 4–5 minutes to fill in the room details under Landlord / Landlady, using their imagination where necessary. Make sure the two students in each pair choose different rooms. When they finish, tell them to read the Tenant section and point out the *Target language*. Tell them to decide who is going to play the role of landlord / landlady first.

**Tip** If all the students have mobile phones, tell them to get them out and to pretend to use them. It makes the conversations and the body language much more realistic.

Elicit how such a telephone conversation is likely to begin (*Hello. I'm phoning about the room…*) and let them start the role play, swapping roles and starting again when they finish. Get some feedback at the end on what they found out and if they all made an appointment successfully.

## Follow-up suggestion

If you have time, or you think students would enjoy doing it in a subsequent lesson, set up a follow-on role play in which the tenants view the flat they've phoned up about. They don't need to stand up to do this. Just give a piece of paper to the landlords / landladies, on which they can sketch a quick plan of the flat. Then they can show the tenant round, using the plan as a prop. Target language might include:

*Here is… (the room). There is (a wardrobe) in the corner. There are (some drawers) next to (the window). This is… (the kitchen).* etc.

# Finding accommodation

**A** **You are looking for a room in Clapham, a part of London, for between £100 and £130 per week. This is what you find on one website. Read the four advertisements and find the words that mean the following:**

a) *Tube* ______ underground railway
b) ______ the price includes bills
c) ______ the price doesn't include bills
d) ______ per week
e) ______ below the ground floor
f) ______ with all the furniture you need
g) ______ with good quality windows
h) ______ modern conveniences (e.g. washing machine, microwave oven, etc.)
i) ______ with lots of space
j) ______ with built-in cupboards
k) ______ the bathroom is in the room

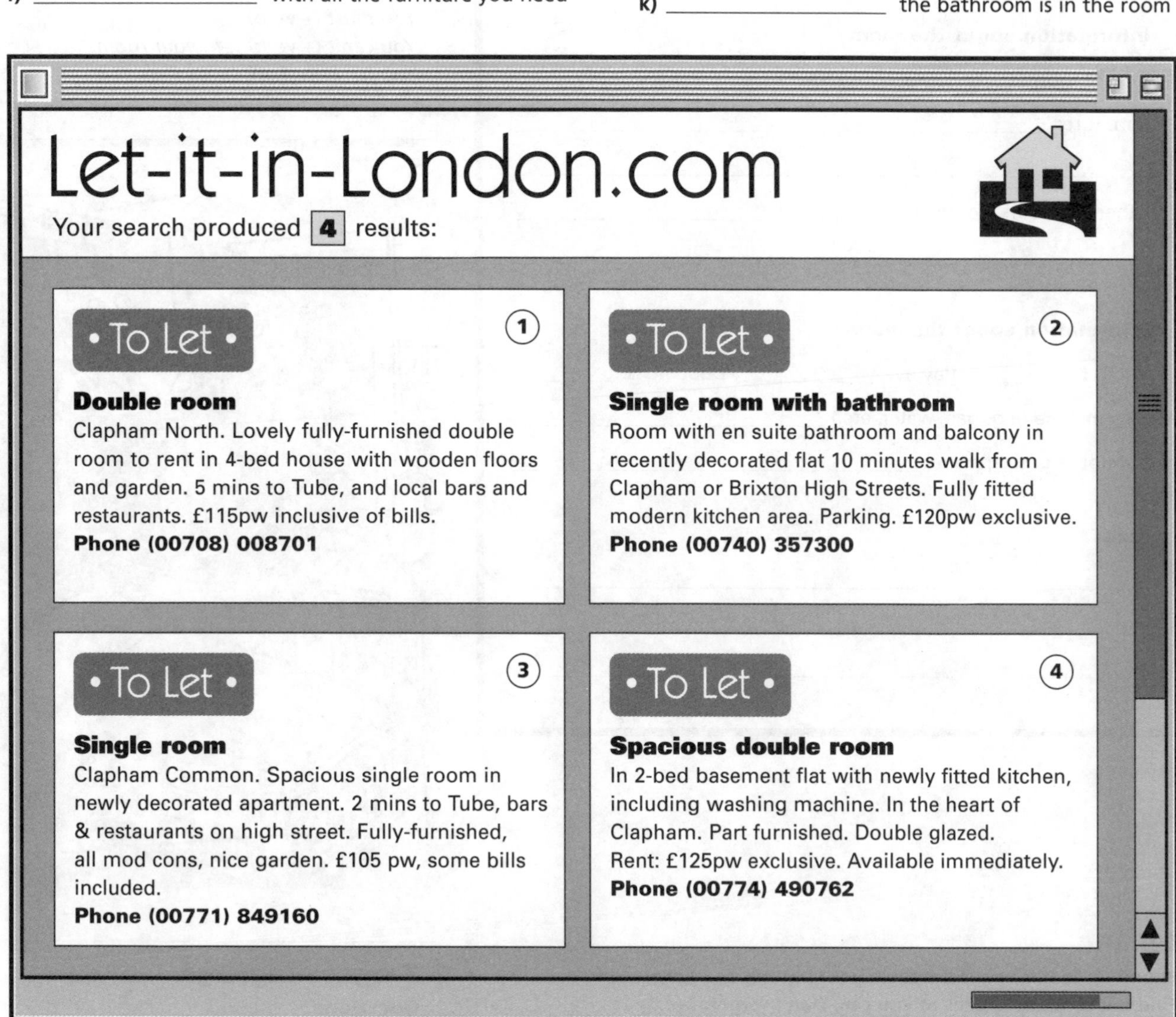
Let-it-in-London.com
Your search produced 4 results:
• To Let • 1
Double room
Clapham North. Lovely fully-furnished double room to rent in 4-bed house with wooden floors and garden. 5 mins to Tube, and local bars and restaurants. £115pw inclusive of bills.
Phone (00708) 008701
• To Let • 2
Single room with bathroom
Room with en suite bathroom and balcony in recently decorated flat 10 minutes walk from Clapham or Brixton High Streets. Fully fitted modern kitchen area. Parking. £120pw exclusive.
Phone (00740) 357300
• To Let • 3
Single room
Clapham Common. Spacious single room in newly decorated apartment. 2 mins to Tube, bars & restaurants on high street. Fully-furnished, all mod cons, nice garden. £105 pw, some bills included.
Phone (00771) 849160
• To Let • 4
Spacious double room
In 2-bed basement flat with newly fitted kitchen, including washing machine. In the heart of Clapham. Part furnished. Double glazed.
Rent: £125pw exclusive. Available immediately.
Phone (00774) 490762

**B** **Now look again at the four advertisements and discuss the advantages and disadvantages of each. Which two would you like to find out more about? What would you like to find out?**

**Write some questions here about the room, the house, details about costs and house rules.**

 

# Finding accommodation



## Landlord / Landlady

**You are the landlord / landlady of one of the two rooms you chose with your partner. Complete the information below. If someone phones you up about the room, be helpful and try to organise an appointment to view the room and the house. If they ask you about something that isn't written below, create your own answer!**

Your Name ______________________________

Address ______ ______________________ Street, Clapham

**Information about the room**

Size of room: ______m x ______m

Furniture: ______________________________

______________________________

Other rooms in the house: ______________________________

______________________________

**Information about the money**

Rent: £ ________ Pay every ________ Deposit: £ ________

Bills include (e.g. gas, water, etc.) ______________________________

but not (e.g. telephone) ______________________________

**Rules**

______________________________

______________________________

______________________________

### Target language

*The room is still available.*
*What would you like to know?*
*There is / are (+ noun) in the room.*
*The size is...*

**Making an appointment**

*Would you like to come and see the house?*
*What about on Monday at 6:30?*

**Obligations and rules**

*You must (+ verb)...*
*You can't (+ verb)... in your room.*
*You have to share the...*
*...isn't / aren't allowed.*

## Tenant

**Phone up to ask about the room your partner has prepared for. Find out as many details as you can. Don't forget:**

- ☑ money – check the rent, cost of bills, etc.
- ☑ room – size, furniture
- ☑ house / flat – rooms, furniture
- ☑ rules – guests, smoking, pets, etc.

**If you are happy with the details, make an appointment to view the flat. Note down the details here:**

Day ______________________ Time ______________________

Address ______________________________

### Target language

**Questions**

*Hello. I'm phoning about the room.*
*Is it still available?*
*How much is...?*
*Does that include...?*
*How big is...?*
*Is there a bed / TV...in the room?*

**Making an appointment**

*Would it be possible to view the room?*
*How about Tuesday?*
*What time is best for you?*
*I'll see you then.*

**Obligations and rules**

*Can I (+ verb)...?*
*Is it possible to (+ verb)...?*

 

# 5a The elixir of life – Teacher's notes

## Time / Level
45–60 minutes / Intermediate to Advanced

## Target language
**Grammar**

Conditionals, esp. first and second (*If you kill me, you won't have anybody to cure your illnesses.*)

Narrative tenses (in the story)

**Functions**

Making and denying accusations (*It was him! I wasn't there. He's lying!*)

Speculating about the future (*If you don't, what will happen?*)

**Vocabulary**

Various, including health (*elixir, eternal youth*), politics (*prime minister*) and punishment

## Preparation
Copy the story *The elixir of life* (one per pair) and the seven role play cards A–G (one per student). Cut up as indicated. Cut up some small slips of paper (one per student) and get some sticky tape for name badges.

Depending on the number of students in your class, you will need to decide how many groups you will have and how many of the role cards you will use. Minimum four students (or three plus the teacher) – use cards A to D. For five, add G. For six, add E and F (leave out G). For seven include all the role cards. For eight or more, create two or more groups.

## Lead-in suggestion
Hand out the story (one per pair) and read it out yourself as the narrator. Use mime and expression in your voice to bring it to life. When they've finished, see if they can guess the meaning of *elixir, magician, eternal youth* and *dose*. Then put them into pairs to discuss the three questions underneath (3 minutes). Get feedback. The students will probably have a lot of creative ideas. Tell them that they are now going to role play the meeting between the king and his friends.

## Role Play instructions
If you haven't already done so, decide how many groups you will have and how many students in each group. Hand out one role play card to each student, choosing yourself who is likely to make the best king (not necessarily a man) and who would suit the other roles. Give them two minutes to read their role and ask you about any vocabulary. As they finish, remind them of the *Target language* on the story sheet and give them a small piece of paper and sticky tape to make themselves a name badge. When they are all ready, sit each group in a tight circle to begin the role play. Let the king start by reading the spoken lines at the end of the story. He then should ask one of the other characters: "Do you know who took the elixir?" Take a back seat until the action gets going and let them decide how to develop the 'plot'. You could make discreet notes on commonly recurring errors for the feedback stage. Depending on the students' level, character and rapport, the role play could last from 15–30 minutes.

## Follow-up suggestion
If you had more than one group, tell the groups to summarise to each other what happened in their role plays, how the plot developed and who the king has decided to punish. If you had just one group, praise them yourself on their performances. If you made notes on recurring mistakes, you can provide feedback on these now.

**Further ideas:** Students may like to turn their role play into a 'real' play, writing a script or improvising it in front of a video camera. Alternatively they could continue and conclude the story, writing from the point of view of their character for homework.

# THE ELIXIR OF LIFE

ONCE upon a time, there lived in ancient China a king called Di Wu. He was very old, some said over 100 years, and very healthy. The secret of his good health was his elixir of life. It had been given to him as a child by a wise magician, who had told him to drink 10 drops every year to keep him young and healthy. He kept the elixir secret from all the people, worried that they might try to steal some of it, and for many years nobody knew the secret of his eternal youth.

Unfortunately, one day when he was drunk on wine he told his closest friends about the elixir. The stories soon spread and everybody in the city began talking about it and started to wonder if it was really the secret of eternal youth. The months passed, and the New Year arrived. Di Wu went to the room where he kept the elixir for his yearly dose. However, when he took the elixir from its box, he noticed that the box had been opened recently, and the bottle inside was empty.

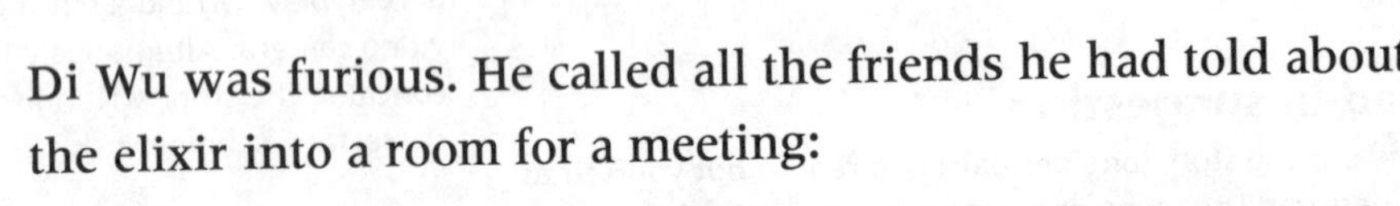

Di Wu was furious. He called all the friends he had told about the elixir into a room for a meeting:

"Several months ago, I told you all about the elixir of life. This morning I found the bottle empty. Somebody has stolen the elixir. If I don't find out who it was, I will kill all of you."

## Discussion

1) What do you think has happened to the elixir?

2) What do you think will happen at the meeting?

3) Do you believe in the power of the elixir?

## Role Play

You will take part in a group role play. You will be one of the people at the meeting. Your teacher will give you a role play card. Read it and think carefully about what you will say. Check the target language before you begin.

### Target language

**Making accusations**

*It was you! She did it!*
*He took it because…*
*I don't trust you / him.*

**Denying accusations**

*It wasn't me. I wasn't there.*
*How can you say that?*
*It's got nothing to do with me.*
*I can explain everything.*

**Conditionals**

*If you tell the truth, I'll… (verb)*
*If you kill me, you'll… (verb)*

 

## The elixir of life Student A – King Di Wu

You are King Di Wu. You are angry and must find out who has drunk your elixir. If more than one person has taken some of the elixir, you should decide who to punish, and how. If anybody has a very good reason for taking it, perhaps you will spare them. You can try to get advice from your friends, but everybody is under suspicion. Start them arguing. That will show who your real friends are. Ask as many questions as you need to.

Start the meeting by reading the spoken line at the end of the story: "Several months ago…" Then ask one of your 'friends': "Do you know who took the elixir?"

***Remember**, you must find at least one person to punish. This will demonstrate your control over the city. If you don't, perhaps your 'friends' will turn against you!*

---

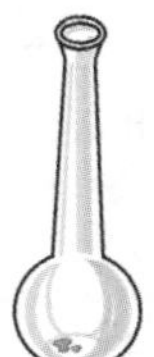

## The elixir of life Student B – Doctor

You are the most respected doctor in the city. Two months ago, you stole 10 drops of the elixir when you were feeling tired and depressed. You have saved a lot of people from death, including the king himself, and you have found the cures to 3 diseases. Thanks to the elixir, you will now be able to save lots more people from death and find cures to more diseases. You know that the politician has also stolen some of the elixir.

---

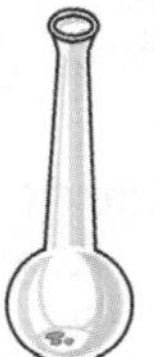

## The elixir of life Student C – Politician

You are the most experienced politician in the city. Three months ago, you stole 10 drops of the elixir when you were feeling sick with heart pains. Since then you have felt much better. You have been Prime Minister for 3 years, and the city has become richer and safer since then. You have improved the hospitals and the schools. You know that the king's wife has also stolen some of the elixir.

---

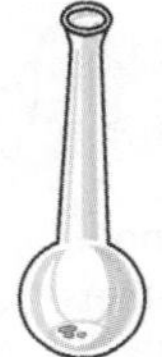

## The elixir of life Student D – King's wife

You are the king's wife. Four months ago, you stole 10 drops of the elixir. You did this because you were worried that you were losing your beauty and that the king would stop loving you. Since then, you have regained your beauty, and the king loves you more than ever. He is happier as a result. You know that the doctor has also stolen some of the elixir.

---

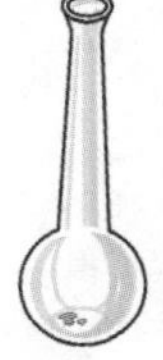

## The elixir of life Student E – Artist

You are the king's artist. Five months ago, you stole 10 drops of the elixir when you were finding it difficult to come up with ideas for your art. Since then, you have had many great ideas, and started the largest and most beautiful painting on the walls of the Town Hall. All the people are very happy with it, and it will be finished in 1 month. You know that the chemist has also stolen some of the elixir.

---

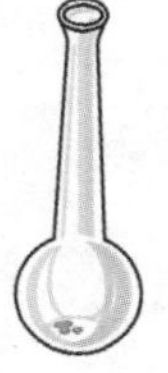

## The elixir of life Student F – Chemist

You are the Professor of Chemistry at the city university. Four months ago, you stole 10 drops of the elixir. You did this because you wanted to understand what it was made from so that you could make more. Unfortunately, you had no success, and so you decided to drink the 10 drops, which have helped you to turn silver into gold, increasing the king's wealth and the beauty of the city. You know that the artist has also stolen some of the elixir.

---

## The elixir of life Student G – General

You are the general of the king's army that protects the city. Two months ago, you stole 10 drops of the elixir. You did this because you were about to fight a war, and needed extra strength and courage. Since then, you have won the war, and increased the territory of the kingdom by another 30 miles. The king never thanked you for this. The soldiers all believe in you, and you don't think the king can order them to punish you. You are scared of nothing, not even death.

 

# 5b Fortune teller – Teacher's notes

## Time / Level

40–60 minutes / Intermediate to Advanced

## Target language

**Grammar**

*Will* and future continuous for prediction (*You will be going on a long journey…*)

Modals of advice (*You should look for the answers inside you.*)

**Functions**

Making predictions (*Nature and children will be the two influences over the next year…*)

Describing personality (*You are adventurous and spontaneous*)

Giving advice and recommendations (*You should look for the answers inside you.*)

**Vocabulary**

Adjectives to describe personality (*generous, spontaneous, energetic*, etc.)

## Preparation

Copy the crossword *Adjectives of Personality* (one per pair), the role play cards A and B (one set per pair) and the tarot cards (one set per pair). Cut up as indicated.

## Lead-in suggestion

Put the following questions on the board for discussion in pairs followed by feedback:

1) *Do you have fortune tellers in your country?*
2) *How do they tell your fortune?*
   *(e.g. palm reading, crystal ball, tarot cards)*
3) *Have you ever been to one? What did he / she say?*
4) *Do you believe that some people can see into the future?*

## Role Play instructions

Hand out the crossword first, one per pair, and give students 5–10 minutes to complete it. Check the answers, drilling pronunciation as necessary.

**Answers**

**Across: 1)** responsible **4)** energetic **9)** temperamental **12)** antisocial **13)** spontaneous **14)** decisive

**Down: 2)** private **3)** unpredictable **5)** sensitive **6)** optimistic **7)** reliable **8)** generous **10)** adventurous **11)** fate

Then introduce the role play, reminding the students that it's just for speaking practice and the advice shouldn't be taken seriously.

Hand out the role play cards. Give *Student A – Visitor* to one student in each pair and *Student B – Fortune Teller* to the other one. Give them 3–5 minutes to read their sheets. During this time, the visitors should choose five adjectives of personality to describe themselves from the crossword, and the fortune tellers should read through the meanings of the cards.

Start the role play when they are ready. Put on some mystic background music to get the right atmosphere and encourage the fortune tellers to improvise and have fun. When each pair has finished their first role play, get the visitor to provide feedback, following the instructions on the sheet. Then swap them over and repeat the whole process.

## Follow-up suggestion

Find out from the students who would make a good professional fortune teller and why, and who would not. Find out how they felt performing the roles and whether anyone is now interested in visiting a real fortune teller.

 

# Fortune teller

## Crossword – Adjectives of Personality

**Complete the crossword with the words from the box, using the clues below.**

| | | | | | | |
|---|---|---|---|---|---|---|
| generous | spontaneous | energetic | antisocial | unpredictable | fate | responsible |
| temperamental | adventurous | decisive | optimistic | reliable | sensitive | private |

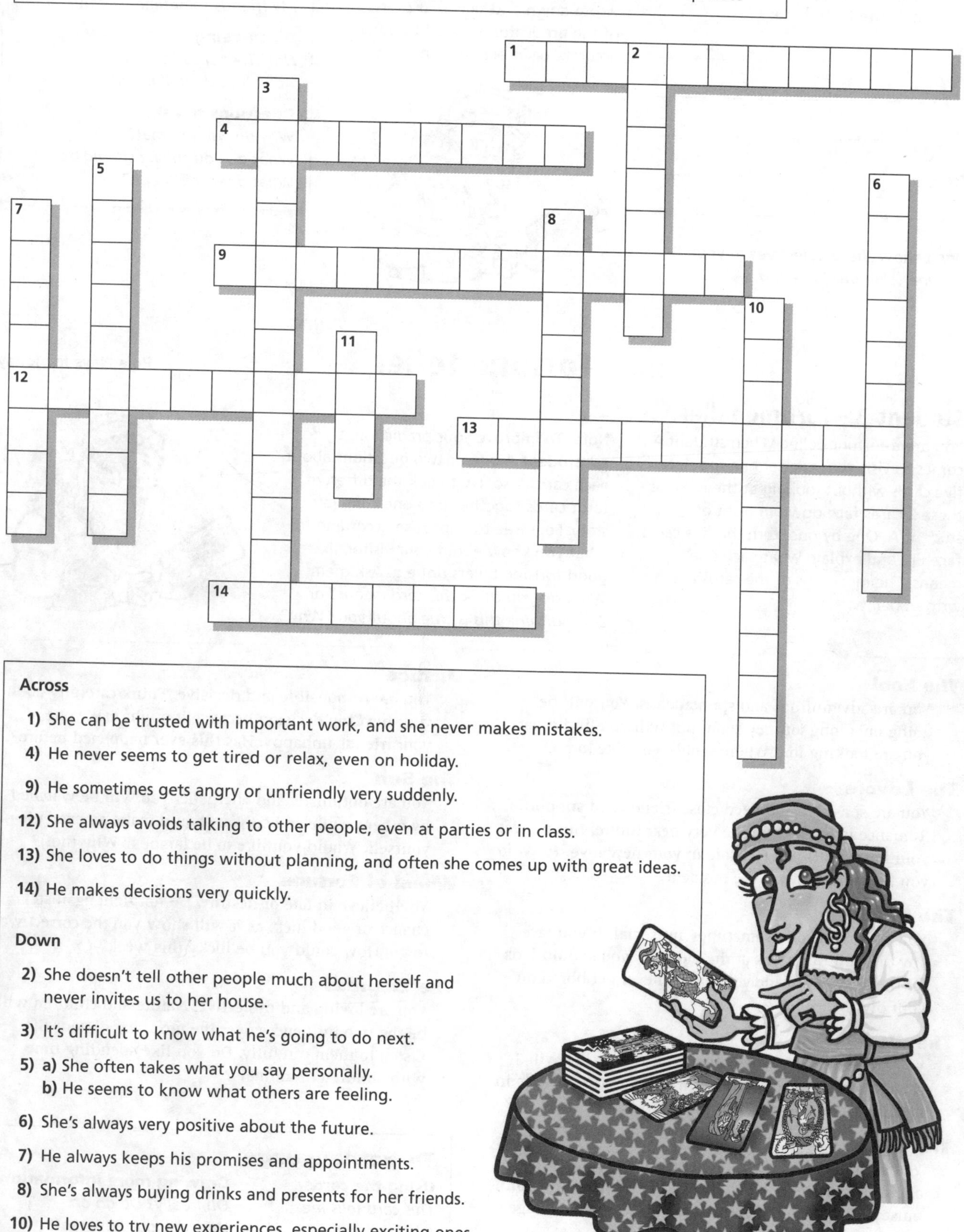


**Across**

1) She can be trusted with important work, and she never makes mistakes.
4) He never seems to get tired or relax, even on holiday.
9) He sometimes gets angry or unfriendly very suddenly.
12) She always avoids talking to other people, even at parties or in class.
13) She loves to do things without planning, and often she comes up with great ideas.
14) He makes decisions very quickly.

**Down**

2) She doesn't tell other people much about herself and never invites us to her house.
3) It's difficult to know what he's going to do next.
5) a) She often takes what you say personally.
   b) He seems to know what others are feeling.
6) She's always very positive about the future.
7) He always keeps his promises and appointments.
8) She's always buying drinks and presents for her friends.
10) He loves to try new experiences, especially exciting ones.
11) (Not an adjective) The idea that your life has already been planned for you (e.g. by God).

# Fortune teller



## Student A – Visitor

You are about to visit a fortune teller to find out about your future. First, choose five adjectives of personality from the crossword you have just done to describe yourself. Write them here:

1) ______________________

2) ______________________

3) ______________________

4) ______________________

5) ______________________

***Don't show these adjectives to your fortune teller until the end.***

Now visit the fortune teller and follow his/her instructions carefully. At the end, show her/him the 5 adjectives you wrote down and say what parts of the prediction seemed to be accurate or interesting and why.

### Target language

**Agreeing**

*Yes. That's very true.*
*My friends sometimes say the same.*

**Disagreeing**

*No! The opposite is true.*
*Actually, I think I'm quite...*

**Questions to ask**

*Why do you say that?*
*What do you think I should do?*
*What does this mean?*

---

# Fortune teller

Role Plays for Today

## Student B – Fortune teller

You are a fortune teller. When student A comes to visit you, ask her/him to select five cards without looking at them. Place these 5 cards face down in front of student A. One by one, turn the five cards face up, and explain what each one means. The meanings of the cards are written below:

Note: To improve your prediction, try to ask student A one or two questions about each card. Also, try to link the different tarot cards together into one complete story. Feel free to improvise according to what you know about your visitor, like all good fortune tellers do! e.g. Ask them: *What do you think this card means?* or *Do you think this is true about you? Why?*

**The Fool**

You are adventurous and spontaneous. You will be going on a long journey soon. But will you find what you are looking for? Where would you like to go?

**The Lovers**

You are sensitive and need close friends and support. Romance is possible in the very near future. But protect your heart until you feel safe in your new love. How do you feel about love at the moment?

**The Hermit**

You are private and sometimes antisocial. If you face any difficult questions at the moment, you should look for the answers inside you. Do you ever get bored on your own?

**The World**

You are generous and reliable. Your role in life will change soon and you will begin to help other people in need. Is there any charity you would like to work for?

**The Tower**

You are unpredictable and temperamental. You are about to experience a big change in your life, and you must prepare yourself for it. Are you scared of change? Why (not)?

**Justice**

You are responsible and decisive. Think carefully about your next big decision because it might make one of your friends unhappy. Has this ever happened before?

**The Sun**

You are optimistic and energetic. You will be watched by other people and so you should make an example of yourself. Would you like to be famous? Why (not)?

**Wheel of Fortune**

You believe in fate or destiny. Do not fight against chance or good luck, as it will show you the correct way to go. How could you be lucky this week?

**The Empress**

You are loving and protective. Nature and children will be the two influences over the next year of your life. Listen to them carefully. Do you like spending time with children or animals?

### Target language

**Using the cards**

*This card tells me...*
*Oh, look at this!*
*This is good news...*
*I can see that you like...*

**Drawing more information**

*Oh, really? Do go on.*
*Why do you think that?*
*What do you think it means?*
*Yes, I know. What else?*
*Is this true?*

The Fool

The Lovers

The Hermit

The World

The Tower

Justice

The Sun

Wheel of Fortune

The Empress

# 5c Interviewing a writer / actor – Teacher's notes

## Time / Level

40–60 minutes / Pre-intermediate to Upper intermediate

## Target language

**Grammar**

Present perfect (esp. simple) to talk about life experience (*I've won over 20 awards.*)

Past simple to provide detail (*I started writing when I was just 14.*)

Question forms (*What happened next?*)

**Functions**

Asking starter questions (*Have you ever had any problems in your life?*)

Asking follow-up questions (*I see. How difficult was that?*)

Showing interest (*Really? Go on.*)

**Vocabulary**

Literature (*novel, influence*) and genres of literature (*science fiction, children's writer*)

Films (*actor, director*) and genres of film (*romance, action*)

## Preparation

Copy role play cards A and B (two sets per pair). Cut up as indicated. Take in some small slips of paper (one per student) for the follow-up suggestion.

## Lead-in suggestion

Pre-teach: *journalist*; *award* if necessary.

Write the following questions on the board for discussion in pairs followed by feedback.

1) *Would you prefer to be a famous actor or a famous writer? Why?*
2) *What would you like / dislike about being famous?*

## Role Play instructions

Introduce the role play by telling the students that today they are going to play the roles of famous actors and writers. Tell each pair to decide who is going to go first, and give out the relevant role play cards. Give them 8–10 minutes to read their cards and prepare for the interview. If necessary, go through an example with the writers / actors:

| **In my life…** | Yes? No? | How many? How much? | Details (what, who, when, where, why, etc.) |
|---|---|---|---|
| *write books* | ✓ | *16* | *1st when 14 – detective story; bestseller 'Love on the Thames' in 2003.* |

Encourage the writers and actors to be creative and let them decide if they want to be a famous celebrity, a fictitious one or themselves in the future. Check that the journalists write appropriate starter questions. Encourage the use of present perfect if you have studied it recently. When they are all ready, let them start the role play. Give them 10–15 minutes. The journalists can start formally: "How do you do? It's an honour to meet you." Monitor. Note down possible errors for correction in the follow up stage.

As the pairs finish, tell them to swap roles and hand out the appropriate role play cards. Repeat the preparation and role play procedure as above.

## Follow-up suggestions

Give each student a slip of paper and tell them to write down three facts about the famous writer / actor they interviewed. Encourage the use of the present perfect if you like. Collect in the pieces of paper and redistribute randomly. Students should read them out to the class, who then try to guess which student played the role of this actor / writer.

Students could be asked to write up a newspaper article of their interview for homework.

# Interviewing an actor or a writer



## Student A – Actor or Writer

You are a famous actor ***or*** writer. A journalist is coming to interview you today about your life. Complete the table before the interview begins. During the interview, use present perfect for life experience and past simple to provide more details.

| In my life... | Yes? No? | How many? How much? | Details (what, who, when, where, why, etc.) |
|---|---|---|---|
| write books | | | |
| make movies | | | |
| win awards | | | |
| make some famous friends | | | |
| live in different countries | | | |
| be married | | | |
| make millions ($) | | | |
| spend millions ($) | | | |
| be poor | | | |
| make mistakes | | | |
| find happiness | | | |

**Target language**

**Talking about your life**

*I have been acting/writing since...*
*I've never..., but I have...*
*I've been to... I've won...*
*I've known... since...*
*I've been married 3 times.*

**Going into detail**

*I started because...*
*I met him when...*
*My problems started when...*
*When I was a child...*

✂-----------------------------------------------------------------------

# Interviewing an actor or a writer

Role Plays for Today

## Student B – Journalist

You are a journalist for 'Sunday Time' newspaper. You have been asked to interview a very famous celebrity. Unfortunately, because of security, nobody knows who it is! It might be a writer or an actor!

Prepare carefully for the interview. Write questions, using the ideas in the box and your own ideas. Use the present perfect to ask about life experience and the past simple to ask for more details.

write books / make films? win awards? make famous friends? live in different countries? be married? have children? make millions ($)? spend millions ($)? make mistakes? find happiness?

1) ______________________________ ?
2) *Have you ever won any awards? When? How did you feel?* ?
3) ______________________________ ?
4) ______________________________ ?
5) ______________________________ ?
6) ______________________________ ?
7) ______________________________ ?
8) ______________________________ ?

**Target language**

**Showing interest**

*Right.*
*Oh, really.*
*That's amazing!*
*Go on, go on.*

**Asking follow-up questions**

*Why was that?*
*When was that?*
*How easy / difficult was that?*
*How did you feel about that?*
*What happened next?*

 

# 5d TV chat show – Teacher's notes

## Time / Level

60–90 minutes / Upper intermediate to Advanced

## Target language

**Grammar**

Passive voice for statistical and factual information (*This can be reduced through education.*)

**Functions**

Expressing your opinion (*I think that…*)

Getting and holding a speaking turn (*Can I just say something?; Sorry. I haven't finished.*)

Appealing to fact (*Actually, that's not true.*)

**Vocabulary**

Crime and punishment (*prison sentence, trial, reoffend, victim of crime*)

Statistics (*2 out of 3, 15% less, decrease*)

## Preparation

This role play works best in classes of 8–20 students, although it could be adapted for use with smaller or larger classes.

Copy the worksheet (one per pair), the *Member of the public* and *Expert* role play cards (2–3 members of the public per expert) the *Oprah* role play card (one copy) and the name badges (one per student). Get hold of a microphone or similar prop for Oprah, and some sticky tape.

## Lead-in suggestion

Ask the students if they have ever seen any chat shows on TV, either American or from their own country. Elicit what usually happens on these shows (*discussion, debate, argument, fighting*) and what kind of topics are usually discussed (*affairs, sex-changes, family fall-outs,* etc.). Tell them that they are going to take part in a similar chat show, but that the topic today will be crime. Hand out the worksheet, one per pair, and tell them to read the five ideas, and then answer the question in A. When they've finished, get feedback.

B) Instruct them to do the vocabulary check.

**Answers**
**1a)** victim of crime **1b)** trial **2a)** (prison) sentence
**2b)** deterred **3a)** the public **3b)** burglary **3c)** armed
**4a)** reoffend **5a)** discipline

Put the students in pairs to do C. It's important for them to formulate and practise expressing their opinion before speaking live on TV (i.e. before the whole class). Don't get feedback. Save it for the show.

## Role Play instructions

Decide yourself on a strong student for the role of Oprah, and give him/her the role play card and the microphone first. Then find out which students feel confident enough to be experts. Ideally, you'll need about one expert for every two or three members of the public. Hand out the appropriate role play cards and give them 2–4 minutes to complete them. Make sure the experts choose different jobs. Monitor, help with vocabulary and point out the *Target language*. Give all the *Members of the public* and the *Experts* a name badge each to complete, and some sticky tape to stick it on with. When the students are ready, rearrange the classroom to create a 'studio floor' in the middle, with the chairs arranged into a circle around the 'floor'. If you have two rows, put the experts on the inside. Put Oprah in the middle and let him/her begin. The role play could last from 20–30 minutes depending on the students.

## Follow-up suggestion

Congratulate all the students and put them into pairs to discuss these questions:

*1) Did you enjoy taking part in the show? Why (not)?*
*2) What did you say? Were you happy with this?*
*3) Did you say everything that you wanted to?*
*4) How did you feel when you were speaking?*
*5) Was there anything anybody said that annoyed you? What did you want to say?*

Get some feedback at the end.

**Idea:** If you think your students would enjoy it and you can get hold of a camera, why not video the show? The students will really enjoy watching the playback. They'll also learn a lot about their pronunciation and errors by watching and listening to themselves.

 

# The Oprah Springer Show

## "How can we reduce crime in society?"

**A** **Read these five ideas about how to reduce crime. Have any of them been suggested or used in your country?**

**Idea 1 – Better education at school**

Children, when they are 14 or 15, meet victims of crime and spend a day with local police officers. They also visit prisons and watch trials taking place.

**Cost:** £30 million per year.

**Evidence for:** 60% of criminals start when they are at school. This can be reduced through education. After meeting victims, 2 out of 3 criminals decided to stop committing crimes.

**Evidence against:** It takes a long time to see any results (10 years). Teachers and police officers would need special training.

**Idea 2 – Longer prison sentences**

Increase the average prison sentences by 20%.
Increase sentences for violent crimes by 40%.

**Cost:** £50 million per year.

**Evidence for:** Fewer criminals on the street. Victims feel satisfied. Criminals might be deterred from committing crimes in the future.

**Evidence against:** Very expensive. More time in prison means the criminals spend more time together which can increase the chance of them reoffending. Also, they have less incentive to behave well if they are in prison for longer.

**Idea 3 – Let the public own guns**

Members of the public are able to defend themselves from crime if they own guns, and they also feel safer.

**Cost:** £0 per year. However, all policemen would need guns as well, which would cost £10 million per year.

**Evidence for:** In some US states, the number of burglaries has fallen as gun ownership has risen. People feel 'safer' in their own homes, especially old people and people in remote villages.

**Evidence against:** More violent crime in the USA than anywhere else in the world, where there is the highest number of guns. Most robbers in the USA are armed. There is a greater risk to the police and a greater risk of serious accidents.

**Idea 4 – Give more help to criminals leaving prison**

Ex-prisoners are given jobs doing local council work. Training is given for these jobs while they are in prison.

**Cost:** £35 million per year.

**Evidence for:** In the UK 50% of criminals who don't receive help reoffend within 1 year of leaving prison. Most complain that they 'couldn't get any other job.' A similar programme in Sweden reduced the number of criminals who reoffend by 25%. Teenagers find the training useful.

**Evidence against:** Some people might commit crimes to get a 'free' job or 'free' training.

**Idea 5 – Introduce 'boot camps'**

Special prisons where criminals are forced to work hard each day, doing useful things. Criminals feel like they are in the army, and learn discipline. Sentences are shorter.

**Cost:** £80 million to build four camps. When opened, the prisoners work to pay for their living costs.

**Evidence for:** In the USA, where boot camps are common, prisoners are 5–15% less likely to reoffend over the next 3 years. Prisoners find it easier to get work after boot camp, often in the army.

**Evidence against:** Some teenagers may become more aggressive after boot camps. Criminals who go to boot camps often get shorter sentences, which may sound easier for some criminals. And do we really want former criminals in the army?

## B Vocabulary check

**Find words in the five ideas that have these meanings. The letters 1–5 refer to the idea numbers:**

**1a)** ________________ (noun) somebody who lost something to a criminal or suffered from crime
**1b)** ________________ (noun) the process where we decide if a person is a criminal or not
**2a)** ________________ (noun) the amount of time a criminal has to go to prison for
**2b)** ________________ (verb) to discourage or convince somebody not to do something
**3a)** ________________ (noun) an expression to refer to people in general, not criminals
**3b)** ________________ (noun) the crime of breaking into somebody's house to steal something
**3c)** ________________ (adj) with a gun or a knife
**4a)** ________________ (verb) when a criminal commits more crime after prison
**5a)** ________________ (noun) strong control or order created by using rules or punishment

## C Pair discussion

**1)** Which of the five solutions seem like good ideas to you?
**2)** Which seem to be good value for money?
**3)** Which do you think are bad ideas? Why?
**4)** Can you think of any other ways to reduce crime?

## D Role Play

**You are now going to take part in a TV chat show on the subject of reducing crime in society.**

# TV chat show



## Member of the public

**You are going to take part in a TV chat show on the following question:**

**"How can we reduce crime in society?"**

**Before you take part, think carefully about your opinion on this subject.**

- Which of the five ideas did you like most?
- What would you like to say on this subject?
- Do you have any other ideas for reducing crime?
- Can you think of any examples from your country to support your arguments?

**Make notes here about your identity. You don't have to use your real name:**

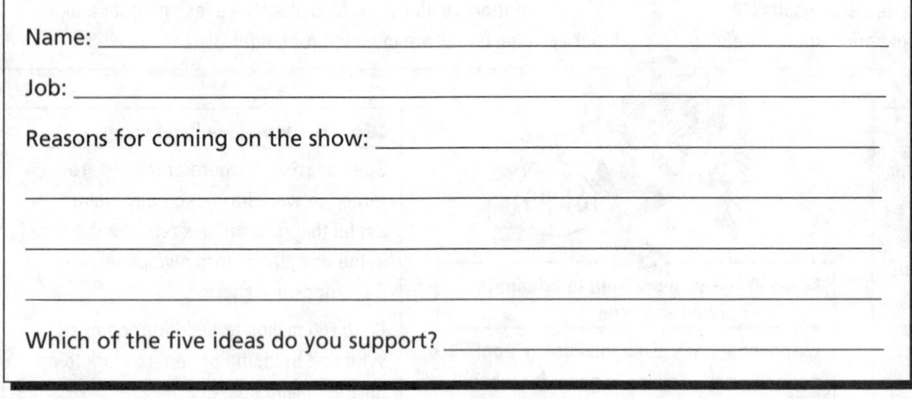

Name: ______________________

Job: ______________________

Reasons for coming on the show: ______________________

Which of the five ideas do you support? ______________________

**Target language**

**Getting the floor**

*I would like to say that...*
*Excuse me, but...*
*I'm sorry, but I can't agree.*
*Can I just say something?*

**Keeping the floor**

*Sorry. I haven't finished.*
*Please don't interrupt.*

**Appealing to fact**

*Actually, that is not true!*
*I read somewhere that...*

**The teacher will give you a name badge. Put your name and job on it. During the show, if you want to speak, put your hand up. If Oprah allows you to speak, stand up.**

# TV chat show



## Expert

**You are going to take part in a TV chat show on the following question:**

**"How can we reduce crime in society?"**

**You are an expert on crime. Choose one of these jobs:**

police officer criminal psychologist judge school teacher
crime writer criminal prison officer gun expert

Name: ______________________

Job: ______________________

**Think carefully about which of the five ideas you support and why.**
**Note down some more facts that will help to make your arguments stronger.**
**You can use your imagination!**

______________________

______________________

______________________

______________________

______________________

**Target language**

**Getting the floor**

*I would like to say that...*
*Excuse me, but...*
*I'm sorry, but I can't agree.*
*Can I just say something?*

**Keeping the floor**

*Sorry. I haven't finished.*
*Please don't interrupt.*

**Appealing to fact**

*Sorry, you don't know that.*
*Believe me. I'm an expert.*
*Actually, that is not true!*
*If you look at the facts...*
*According to research...*

**The teacher will give you a name badge to complete. During the show, if you want to speak, put your hand up. But you don't have to stand up to speak. You are an expert!**

 

# TV chat show

## Oprah Springer

You are Oprah Springer, the famous TV chat show host! You are going to lead a show on the topic of reducing crime in society. There will be both experts and members of the general public in the room. Start like this:

> **How can we reduce crime in modern society? If we had £100 million of government money to spend on reducing crime in the UK, what would we spend it on? That is the question we are going to answer today on the Oprah Springer Show. In the studio we have experts and members of the public. Prime Minister, are you watching?**

Then ask an expert for their opinion. Next ask the members of the public if they agree or disagree. This should lead into a long discussion. Try to balance the two sides of the discussion by choosing carefully who speaks next. Refer back to the five ideas you looked at if you need to get the discussion going again:

> **So, is there anybody here who thinks that boot camps are a good idea?**

Keep people calm if they get angry, and summarise what people say if it's not too clear. The show is planned to last for 20 minutes. At the end, finish the show like this:

> **So, you've heard a great range of opinions on the topic of reducing crime in modern society. Have any of them convinced you to do something, Prime Minister? I hope so. That's all we have time for on today's show. We'll see you next week. Bye.**

**Target language**

**Asking for opinion**

*What do you think on the subject?*
*Do you agree with him?*
*Has anybody ever been a victim of crime?*
*What's your opinion, sir / madam?*
*Why do you think that?*
*Does anybody disagree with her?*
*Sorry. What's your occupation?*

**Controlling the audience**

*Don't interrupt please!*
*Just calm down, please!*
*Could you speak louder, please?*
*I don't understand your point.*
*Could you finish there, please?*

---

| The Oprah Springer Show | The Oprah Springer Show |
|---|---|
| **Name:** ______ | **Name:** ______ |
| **Job:** ______ | **Job:** ______ |

| The Oprah Springer Show | The Oprah Springer Show |
|---|---|
| **Name:** ______ | **Name:** ______ |
| **Job:** ______ | **Job:** ______ |

| EXPERT | EXPERT |
|---|---|
| **Name:** ______ | **Name:** ______ |
| **Job:** ______ | **Job:** ______ |

# 5e Political debate – Teacher's notes

## Time / Level

50–70 minutes / Intermediate to Advanced

## Target language

**Grammar**

Mixed, possibly including future verb structures and verb patterns (*...want to reduce...*, etc.)

**Functions**

Expressing (group) opinion (*We believe that...*)
Agreeing and disagreeing (*We disagree with the... party on the issue of...*)

**Vocabulary**

Politics and government (*policy, taxes, ban*)
The environment (*greenhouse gases, pollution, green transport*)

## Preparation

Copy the three role play cards (2–3 copies per team) and cut up as indicated. If you have a class of over 16 students, consider having two debates in two groups.

## Lead-in suggestion

Introduce the role play to the students – a political debate in which they will play the roles of politicians from three fictitious parties. Write the names of the three political parties from the role play on the board. Explain or elicit *policies* and ask the students:

*From the name, what do you think is important to each party? What are their main policies?*

Give the students 5 minutes to discuss ideas in pairs or small groups. Get feedback and build up lists under each party name. See the role play cards for basic answers. Students may have many more.

Now ask the students to decide which of the three parties they would be most likely to join. If possible, put them all into their preferred party, but you may have to coax some of them to change parties to ensure you have three groups of roughly the same size. Write their names on the board below their party name and reseat the party members together to start the role play.

## Role Play instructions

Tell the students that the political debate will start in 15 minutes. But first they must prepare. Write the question for the debate on the board:

*What can the government do to reduce pollution (including greenhouse gases) and to improve the environment over the next 10 years?*

Ensure all the students understand (you may have to explain *greenhouse gases*), then hand out the role play cards (2–3 copies per team, depending on student numbers). Let them read the cards and begin preparing. Monitor. Make sure they notice the *Target language* for expressing party opinion.

After 15 minutes, arrange the seats into a large circle if possible, and tell the students that you will 'chair' the debate.

**Note:** If you have two groups, it will be necessary to have two students play the role of 'chair' and monitor between the two groups yourself.

Start with the first bullet point on the cards: *taxes on buying cars / petrol* and invite each party to voice its opinion. Once all three parties have stated their point of view, one or two speakers will want to add more. Allow each point to develop appropriately, but try to avoid it becoming a free-for-all! Continue through all the bullet points in a similar manner. The time for the debate will vary from 20–30 minutes. To conclude, recap on what key points have been made / agreed upon, and say that these will be proposed in the recommendation to the government.

## Follow-up suggestion

Tell the students to think back and note down ideas, words or expressions in their first language that they weren't able to express in English during the heat of the debate. Tell them to work alone or in pairs for a few minutes, using dictionaries if necessary, to translate or construct these ideas in English. Monitor. At the end, write some of the more useful sentences onto the board for all the students to note down.

# Political debate



## Group A – The People party

**You believe in providing services for the people of the country. Public transport can be improved (buses, trains, Tube and tram systems), which will help people to travel to work and shops without doing so much damage to the environment.**

Decide what points you are going to make in the debate, and who will make them. Think about:

- taxes on buying cars / petrol
- the price of public transport for different people
- the quality of public transport services
- green transport (bicycles, electric cars)
- improvements in technology, allowing people to shop and work from home
- pollution from factories and power stations

Try to guess what the other parties will say, and how you can respond to their claims. The Profit party believe in economic growth (capitalism) before everything else. The Green party believe in the environment before everything else.

**Target language**

*We believe that…*
*We disagree with the … party.*
*In our opinion…*
*It depends on / what / if…*
*Our main priority is to (verb)…*
*Firstly, we would like to…*
*Secondly, it is important that…*
*What's more, the people of this country want…*
*We propose that the government reduce / increase / ban…*

# Political debate



## Group B – The Profit party

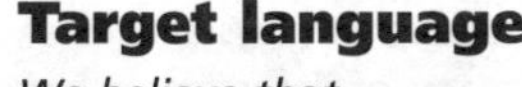

**You believe in improving the economic growth of the country. For this you need to allow people to travel far and wide as much as they need. People need their own cars, and public transport is terrible at the moment.**

Decide what points you are going to make in the debate, and who will make them. Think about:

- taxes on buying cars / petrol
- the price of public transport for different people
- the quality of public transport services
- green transport (bicycles, electric cars)
- improvements in technology, allowing people to shop and work from home
- pollution from factories and power stations

Try to guess what the other parties will say, and how you can respond to their claims. The People party believe in providing services for the people of the country before everything else. The Green party believe in the environment before everything else.

**Target language**

*We believe that…*
*We disagree with the … party.*
*In our opinion…*
*It depends on / what / if…*
*Our main priority is to (verb)…*
*Firstly, we would like to…*
*Secondly, it is important that…*
*What's more, the people of this country want…*
*We propose that the government reduce / increase / ban…*

# Political debate



## Group C – The Green party

**You believe that the environment must come first. If not, there will be no future for anybody. Public transport is better than private cars for reducing pollution, but green transport (bicycles, electric cars) is even better. People need to work nearer to home and shop locally.**

Decide what points you are going to make in the debate, and who will make them. Think about:

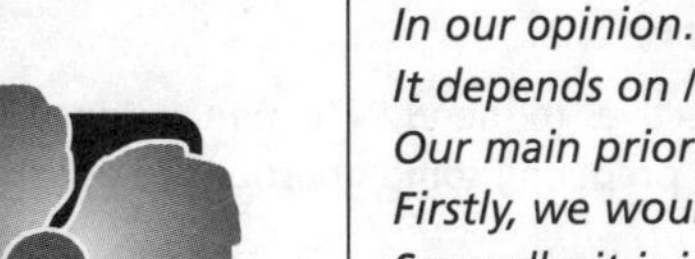

- taxes on buying cars / petrol
- the price of public transport for different people
- the quality of public transport services
- green transport (bicycles, electric cars)
- improvements in technology, allowing people to shop and work from home
- pollution from factories and power stations

Try to guess what the other parties will say, and how you can respond to their claims. The People party believe in providing services for the people of the country before everything else. The Profit party believe in economic growth (capitalism) before everything else.

**Target language**

*We believe that…*
*We disagree with the … party.*
*In our opinion…*
*It depends on / what / if…*
*Our main priority is to (verb)…*
*Firstly, we would like to…*
*Secondly, it is important that…*
*What's more, the people of this country want…*
*We propose that the government reduce / increase / ban…*

# 5f Murder in Paradise – Teacher's notes

## Time / Level

50–70 minutes / Upper intermediate to Advanced

## Target language

**Grammar**

Modal verbs of deduction, present and past (*He couldn't have killed him because...*)

Reported speech / reporting verbs (*He said that you were in the kitchen...*)

**Functions**

Expressing uncertainty (*I'm not sure...*)

**Vocabulary**

Crime (*murder, suspect, motive, alibi*)

## Preparation

This role play works best with larger classes of more than nine, but can also be done with smaller classes successfully.

**9–20 students = 3 or 4 teams of detectives**

4 students (or 3 + teacher) to play the 4 roles and 3 or 4 detective teams of 2–4 students each.

If there are more than 20 students, create 2 groups.

**3–8 students = 1 or 2 teams of detectives**

The teacher plays all 4 roles, and the students work as 1 or 2 teams of detectives, all interviewing you together.

Copy the *Murder in Paradise* worksheet (one per team of detectives, and one for each of the 4 characters), and the 4 character role play cards (one of each). Cut up as indicated.

## Lead-in suggestion

Explain the expression 'murder mystery' to the students and write on the board. Elicit examples of writers (*Agatha Christie, Conan Doyle*) or famous detectives (*Holmes, Poirot*) from the students. Find out if such mysteries are popular in their country / countries, and whether they think they are good at solving them. Tell them that they are going to take part in a murder mystery.

## Role Play instructions

Depending on student numbers (see above), decide who is going to play which of the four characters in the story (choose four strong students), and how many teams of detectives you are going to have. Separate the four characters and sit them together. Hand out a copy of the *Murder in Paradise* worksheet to each team of detectives, and a copy to each of the four characters. Read through the introduction with them.

Teach / Check the following vocabulary: *stab, moan, suspect, motive, alibi.*

Tell the detectives to spend 7–10 minutes discussing possible motives and preparing some questions to ask the suspects.

Meanwhile, give the four characters their role play cards to read and ask them to stick to the story on their role play cards as much as possible. They can refer to their cards if they forget. Point out the *Target language* to all the students. After 10 minutes, they will all be ready to start the interviews.

**If you have 3 or 4 teams of detectives...**

Put each suspect in a corner of the room, and tell the detectives to move around the room, interviewing the suspects one by one.

**If you have 1 or 2 teams of detectives...**

Play the roles of the four characters yourself. Put a chair in the middle of the class, and let them interview you.

The role play will probably take from 30–45 minutes to complete. They may want to interview one suspect several times. If, at any time, a team is waiting to interview a suspect, tell them to discuss who they think the murderer is. When they have finished give them 5–10 minutes to prepare to present their version of events. First find out who each team thinks the murderer is, then ask each team when and why.

**The solution**

Pedro murdered Joel at 9:30 when he went to wash the dishes. He was paid $200,000 by Nigel, who wanted to frame Gillian and Alberto who were having an affair behind Joel's back. With Gillian and Alberto in jail for murder, Nigel would take control of the company. Gillian didn't go to check on Joel at 10, she went to Alberto's room to leave a secret note, so she didn't discover the body! The only clue that points to Pedro is the unwashed knife, as he washed the dishes after he murdered Joel, and before Gillian or Alberto left the lounge.

## Follow-up suggestion

If none of the students guessed the correct murderer and reason, get the characters to explain what really happened, starting with Alberto, then Gillian, then Pedro, then Nigel. If they got the correct murderer, but omitted any important details, elicit these from the characters. If they got it completely correct, get them to tell the other teams how they did it.

**Idea** This role play can be used for a multi-class or whole school social activity. Create more teams of detectives, and get teachers to play the four roles. A little fancy dress and some prizes make it even better.

# Murder in Paradise

## The story so far...

**Joel Arnheim was one of the three owners of a multi-million dollar computer software company. He owns Paradise Island, a luxury Caribbean holiday resort, where he, his wife and his two business partners have been staying for a short holiday. Last night, however, he was murdered!**

**At 9:15pm, Joel went to bed, saying he had a headache. He was discovered by Alberto Rossi at 10:15pm moments before his death. He had been stabbed in his bed, the knife still in his chest. The murderer must be one of the four people who were on the island.**

Pedro, the butler and chef

Gillian Arnheim, Joel's wife

Joel Arnheim MURDERED!

Nigel Palmer, Joel's business partner

Alberto Rossi, Joel's business partner

### Your task

**You are the police detectives. Your task is to interview all these four people and to decide who you think the murderer is. You should present your theory, answering these questions:**

**A)** Who is the murderer?

**B)** When was Joel murdered?

**C)** Why was he murdered?

Pool

Lounge and Dining room

Patio

Kitchen

Reception

Alberto Rossi's room

THE BODY

Joel and Gillian Arnheim's room

Nigel Palmer's room

**The knife** was an unwashed chopping knife. Only Pedro's fingerprints were found on it. But he's the chef!

**The body** had no clues on it. He had been stabbed in the chest once. He was wearing his dressing gown.

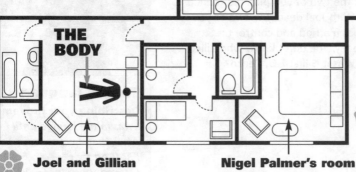

### Target language

*When did you last see Joel alive?*
*Where were you at...?*
*What were you doing?*
*And why did you do that?*
*Did you see anybody else?*
*Do you get on with...?*
*Did you notice...*
*...anything strange?*
*...any arguments between...?*
*Do they get on well?*
*Who do you think killed Joel Arnheim? Why?*

# Murder in Paradise

## Student A – Pedro

### What happened?

*(keep the underlined sentences secret)*

You are the murderer. After dinner, at about 9:15pm Joel went to bed, saying he had a headache. You left everyone in the lounge and went to wash the dishes at about 9:30. You put the dishes in the kitchen quickly, took a big knife, went to the bedroom, stabbed Joel, came back to the kitchen. You washed the dishes and at 9:45, you went back to the lounge to serve drinks from the cocktail bar for all the guests. At 10 o'clock, Gillian left the room to go to see Joel. Surprisingly, she came back 5 minutes later and said he was fine! Then at 10:15, Alberto went to the bathroom, and five minutes later, you all heard him scream. You all ran to find Alberto in Joel's bedroom. Joel was still not dead. The knife was in his chest. He was moaning with pain, too weak to speak, and died a few minutes later.

### What's your secret?

*(don't tell anyone this)*

Your reason for killing Joel is money. Yesterday, Nigel paid you $200,000 to do it. He told you to make it look like Alberto or Gillian killed Joel. Alberto and Gillian have been having a secret love affair. If the police find out about this love affair, they will think that Alberto and Gillian planned the murder to get married and take control of the company. No-one will ever guess it was you who killed Joel! Good luck.

Your only mistake was that you didn't wash the knife before you stabbed Joel. But did anyone else notice that it was dirty?

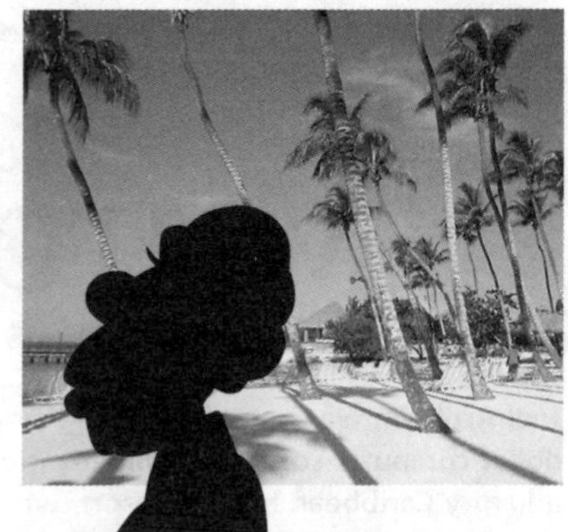

### Target language

**Describing your movements**

*I was in the lounge until (+ time)*
*After that, I went to...*
*I noticed that...*
*I stayed there for (+ time)*
*I heard / saw someone...*

**When you're not sure**

*I can't remember exactly...*
*It was about 10:15...*
*...but I'm not sure...*
*It took just a few minutes.*
*Oh, yes. I forgot...*


# Murder in Paradise


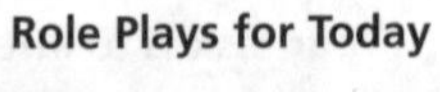


## Student B – Alberto

### What happened?

*(keep the underlined sentences secret)*

You did not kill Joel. After dinner, at 9:15pm Joel went to bed, saying he had a headache. The rest of you were in the lounge. At about 9:30, Pedro went to wash the dishes, as he usually did. He came back about 15 minutes later.
At 10 o'clock, Gillian told everyone she wanted to see how Joel was, so she left the room and came back 5 minutes later, saying he was fine. You wanted to go to your room at 10:15, so you told everyone you were going to the bathroom. You went to your room, where you found a note from Gillian about your meeting tomorrow (you are having a secret love affair with Gillian), then as you left your room, you heard a loud groan from Joel's room. You went to see how he was, and found him dying in bed, with a knife in his chest and blood all over him. He was too weak to speak. You screamed, and everybody came running to see what happened. A few minutes after they arrived, Joel died.

### What's your secret?

*(try to keep this secret if you can)*

You and Gillian have been having a secret love affair. This is why you left the lounge to collect the note that Gillian left for you. But, if you tell the police about your love affair, they will think the two of you planned to kill Joel. With Joel dead, the two of you can get married and control the company. You don't know who killed Joel. Was it Gillian? Or Pedro?

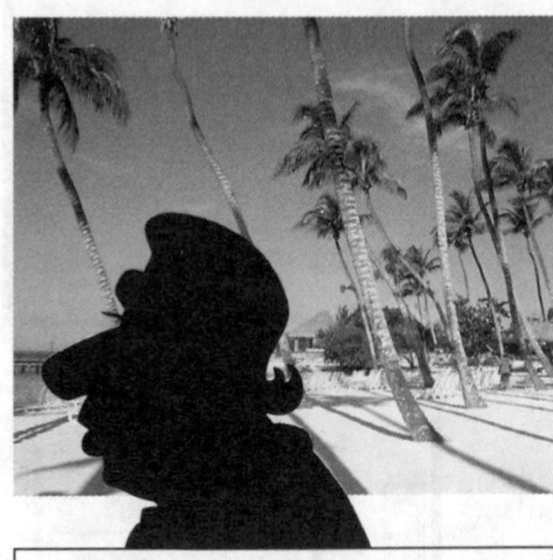


### Target language

**Describing your movements**

*I was in the lounge until (+ time)*
*After that, I went to...*
*I noticed that...*
*I stayed there for (+ time)*
*I heard / saw someone...*

**When you're not sure**

*I can't remember exactly...*
*It was about 10:15...*
*...but I'm not sure...*
*It took just a few minutes.*
*Oh, yes. I forgot...*


 

# Murder in Paradise



## Student C – Gillian

**What happened?**
*(keep the underlined sentences secret)*

You did not kill Joel. After dinner, at 9:15pm Joel went to bed, saying he had a headache. The rest of you were in the lounge. At about 9:30, Pedro went to wash the dishes, as he usually did. He came back about 15 minutes later to serve drinks from the cocktail bar. At 10 o'clock, you told everyone you wanted to see how Joel was, so you left the room. However, you didn't go to see Joel, you went to Alberto's room where you wrote him a note. You came back to the lounge 5 minutes later, and told everyone that Joel was fine – sleeping peacefully. Then at 10:15, Alberto went to his room (to collect your note), and five minutes later, you all heard him scream. You all ran to find Alberto in Joel's bedroom. Joel was still not dead. The knife was in his chest. He was moaning with pain, too weak to speak, and died a few minutes later.

**What's your secret?**
*(try to keep this secret if you can)*

You and Alberto are having a secret love affair. The reason you didn't go to see Joel was because you wanted to leave Alberto a note in his room to organise a meeting for tomorrow. But, if you tell the police this, they will think you and Alberto planned to kill Joel. With Joel dead, the two of you can get married and control the company. You don't know who killed Joel. Was it Alberto? Or Pedro?

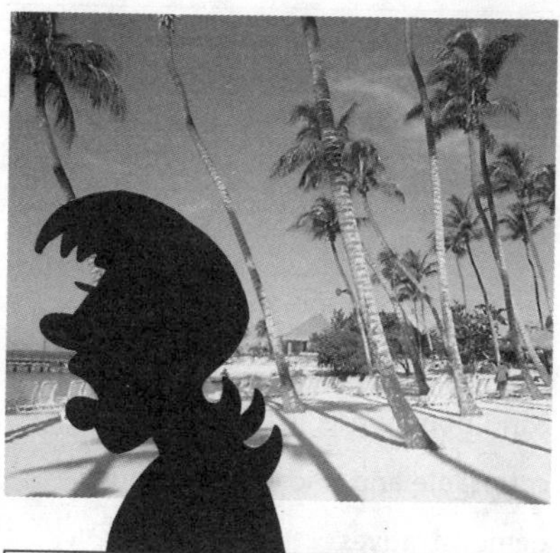

**Target language**

**Describing your movements**
*I was in the lounge until (+ time)*
*After that, I went to...*
*I noticed that...*
*I stayed there for (+ time)*
*I heard / saw someone...*

**When you're not sure**
*I can't remember exactly...*
*It was about 10:15...*
*...but I'm not sure...*
*It took just a few minutes.*
*Oh, yes. I forgot...*

---

# Murder in Paradise



## Student D – Nigel

**What happened?**
*(don't lie about this)*

You were in the lounge all evening, and somebody was with you all the time. After dinner, at 9:15pm Joel went to bed, saying he had a headache. The rest of you were in the lounge. At about 9:30, Pedro went to wash the dishes, as he usually did. He came back about 15 minutes later. At 10 o'clock, Gillian went to see how Joel was, and came back 5 minutes later. Then at 10:15, Alberto went to the bathroom and five minutes later you all heard him scream. You all ran to find Alberto in Joel's bedroom. Joel was still not dead. The knife was in his chest. He was moaning with pain, too weak to speak, and died a few minutes later.

**What's your secret?**
*(you must keep this secret)*

You are confident that no-one will guess the truth. However, secretly, yesterday, you paid Pedro $200,000 to kill Joel. You are not sure, but you think Pedro killed Joel when he went to wash the dishes at 9:30. He came back at about 9:45, looking quite pleased.

When you paid Pedro, you told him to make it look like Alberto or Gillian killed Joel. This is because Gillian and Alberto have been having a secret love affair. This gives them a motive for killing Joel – to be able to marry, and take control of the company together. If they go to prison for the murder, the company is yours!!! Good luck. Don't tell the police about their secret affair too soon. See if the police can find out for themselves!

**Target language**

**Describing your movements**
*I was in the lounge until (+ time)*
*After that, I went to...*
*I noticed that...*
*I stayed there for (+ time)*
*I heard / saw someone...*

**When you're not sure**
*I can't remember exactly...*
*It was about 10:15...*
*...but I'm not sure...*
*It took just a few minutes.*
*Oh, yes. I forgot...*

# Index

## Grammar



## Vocabulary

## Functions

# ROLE PLAYS FOR TODAY

## Photocopiable activities to get students speaking


**Written by** Jason Anderson

**Edited by** Xanthe Sturt Taylor

**Designed by** Christine Cox

**Artwork by** Stephen Lillie

**Photos by** Hemera



**Published by** DELTA Publishing
ADDRESS FOR CORRESPONDENCE
The Editor
DELTA Publishing
Quince Cottage
Hoe Lane
Peaslake
Surrey GU5 9SW
England

Email: info@deltapublishing.co.uk
www.deltapublishing.co.uk

First printed 2006
Reprinted 2011, 2012





Printed in Greece by Bakis

ISBN 1 900783 99 1
ISBN 978 1 900783 99 6